FEDERICO GARCIA
LORCA

O
Outlines

FEDERICO GARCIA
LORCA

DAVID JOHNSTON

Absolute Press

First published in 1998 by Absolute Press
Scarborough House, 29 James Street West,
Bath, Somerset, England BA1 2BT
Tel: 01225 316013 Fax: 01225 445836
Email: sales@absolute press.demon.co.uk

Distributed in the United States of America and Canada by
Stewart, Tabori and Chang
115 West 18th Street, New York, NY 10011

Series editor Nick Drake

Printed by The Cromwell Press, Trowbridge
Covers printed by Devenish and Co. Bath
Cover and text design by Ian Middleton

ISBN 1 899791 61 2

Contents

VIRGIN OF THE SEVEN SORROWS BY FEDERICO GARCÍA LORCA

Preface

For a number of years the English cultural establishment paid little more than
lip-service to the 'genius' of Federico García Lorca. Given that his plays were
rarely performed here and that the only readily-available English-language
editions of his plays and poems contained some of the most excruciating
translations ever to see print, it seems apparent that the accolade of 'genius'
was given on the strength of hearsay, amounting in some cases to little more
than pastiche. In this sense, 1986, the fiftieth anniversary of Lorca's death,
marked a more significant moment than 1998, the centenary of his birth. For
in 1986 international copyright was lifted on those works published in his
lifetime. The lifting was brief, in that international copyright has now been
revised to cover a seventy rather than fifty-year period, but the window of
opportunity was enough to allow for a stream of new translations of a
smattering of his plays and one or two anthologies of poetry. Since then,
however, the Lorca Estate has been much more generous and far-sighted in
its policy of licensing new translations. The result is that in the last decade
Lorca has been firmly established across the English-language cultures as one
of the most performed of foreign dramatists, and if the word 'genius' is still
applied, it is not in that dismissive English way of referring to a foreigner
whose work we think we should know, but don't, but as a genuine
description of a man who produced some of the most powerful plays and
poetry written this century.

Not that Lorca is, as yet, all that well known in this country. Without doubt,
there are two segments of his work – the great trilogy of plays he wrote in
the 1930s, *Blood Wedding*, *Yerma* and *The House of Bernarda Alba*, as well as *Poet
in New York* – which have attracted much attention, and have been elevated to

the status of modern classics. These plays, as well as *Doña Rosita the Spinster*, *The Shoemaker's Wonderful Wife*, *The Love of Don Perlimplín* and, to a lesser extent, *The Public*, *When Five Years Pass* and *Play Without a Title* have now become so entrenched within our theatrical repertoire that Lorca seems to be in continuous performance the length and breadth of the land. Good selections of his poems, from the early *Book of Poems* through *Gypsy Ballads*, one of the best loved books of poetry in the Spanish language, to the final *Sonnets of Dark Love* are also readily available. But those with inside knowledge still like to refer to his other plays and poems as the work of the 'unknown Lorca', although even that epithet is reductionist because there are many Lorcas, many other voices which he raised across a body of work which is remarkable in terms of its commitment to experimentation and to change.[1] The present book contains discussion of most of his plays and poetry, on the basis that one cannot separate Lorca's life from his work. It is impossible to choose a segment of Lorca's work which is representative of the whole, and it is equally impossible to understand the man who created the work, who sang and raged and escaped and dreamed through that work, without reference to the whole of that life.

This is not to say that the book suggests that everything Lorca ever wrote is autobiographical, or can be explained only by reference to his personal circumstances. There is no simple relationship between biography and creativity. It is therefore not quite a literary biography, but, hopefully, it may serve to introduce the man and his writings to those who perhaps know little about either. To that end, all titles and quotations given are in English, in my own translation. Perhaps I should say that these translations endeavour to be both beautiful and faithful, something I have always felt that translations can rarely consistently be. And where I have had to choose between beauty and faithfulness, I have, on this occasion at least, gone for fidelity. I trust the reader will both forgive the resultant infelicities and lay them squarely at my door. But it did seem best to me that the book should offer as accurate an idea as possible of what Lorca had written, without actually simply photocopying his writing into English.

I have adopted throughout, almost unconsciously in the first few instances, the Spanish custom of referring to Lorca as both 'Federico' and 'Lorca'. The reader should not imply anything other than a desire for stylistic variation from the use of the first name. Although I must admit that I have always been touched by this way of referring to a writer now more than sixty years dead, as though he were permanently young. It is an honour which in the Spanish-speaking world is generally only reserved for great footballers.

I have taught, translated and talked Lorca for many years now. It would be impossible to name here all those people who have impressed and influenced me with an insight into his mind and work which goes far beyond mine. This book owes many debts of gratitude, however, and I am glad to be able to acknowledge them here. I am grateful to Bill Kosmas for his kindness and support similarly to Nick Drake who edited the book with both passion and precision, and the other to Paul Fagan who ably read between the lines. Two other people stand out in my memory. One is Gerry Mulgrew, who directed a ground-breaking *Blood Wedding* for Communicado in 1988, and whose own sense of *duende* is as close to Lorca's own as any I've ever come across. The other is an old man, whose name I never did discover, who allowed me into the Huerta de San Vicente in Granada about a year before it was officially opened as the Lorca House-Museum. As we came down the stairs from the bedroom where Lorca had written *Blood Wedding*, my unofficial guide looked out of the window and pointed out where he had lived nearby as a child. He remembered the notoriously sweet-toothed Lorca coming up to his house nearly every day because his mother made the finest cakes for miles around. Then brushing a tear from his eye, he said simply: 'Federico... ¡ay, qué pena!'[2]

David Johnston

Belfast, August 1998

LORCA PLAYING THE PIANO, GRANADA, 1935

Introduction

The Two Federicos

Federico García Lorca is Spain's best known twentieth-century writer, arguably the country's most distinctive modern voice. He was also extraordinarily prolific and multifaceted, producing an astonishing range of work - prose, poetry, plays, essays, drawings and music - which has long been the object of critical analysis and heated cultural debate. Moreover, the circumstances of his death - his appalling murder at the hands of Nationalist insurgents in his own native Granada just as the Civil War was beginning – have also cast their own morbid but lingering spell over his work. It is probably the darkly powerful attraction of Lorca's fate, in contrast with the ebullience of his personality, as well as the richly imagistic, deeply evocative nature of his writing, which have made of him the inspiration both for a myriad of devised pieces, operas, films, poetry and plays, as well as a rather more sober string of books, articles and reviews.

From these numerous representations and analyses emerge two broadly different (but not always wholly unconnected) versions of Lorca and his work. The first is inspired by the colourful folkloric aura and tragic sense which surround Lorca's life. A typical and far-reaching view in that respect is that of Vicente Aleixandre, a close friend of Lorca's in the 1920s and 1930s, a great poet in his own right and eventual recipient of the Nobel Prize for Literature in 1977 (an award made symbolically on the fiftieth anniversary of the Generation of '27, of which Lorca was a key member). In 1937 Aleixandre remembered his lost friend in these much-quoted words:

Federico passed magically through life, without ever pausing for breath; he came and went before the gaze of his friends like winged genius dispensing its grace, bringing pleasure on his appearance and taking the light away with him again on his departure; Federico seemed above all else the powerful enchanter, the dissipator of sadness and sorrow, casting spells of happiness, conjuring joy, dominating the shadows, which he dispelled with his very presence [...] But his heart was not a happy one. He was capable of all the happiness in the universe; but in the deepest core of his being, perhaps like all great poets, he knew no real happiness. Those who watched him pass through life like a wonderfully coloured bird never really knew him. His heart was capable of the rarest passion, and his being was ennobled by his unending capacity for love and suffering. He loved greatly, a quality which those who knew him least denied that he possessed. And he suffered greatly, he suffered because of love. And that was something probably nobody ever realised.[1]

The other approach is more markedly scholarly, more concerned to tease out textual intricacies, to elucidate theoretical and thematic readings. Both approaches have, of course, produced memorable work, genuinely illuminating of the Lorca they choose to depict. The Ballet Rambert's visually stunning *Cruel Garden* (revived in 1998 to celebrate the centenary of Lorca's birth) and the radical and perceptive analyses of a scholar of the stature of Paul Julian Smith are fine examples of both strands.[2] Somewhere between these two approaches is the scholarly biography and masterly literary detective work of Ian Gibson, the writer who has perhaps done most to rescue Lorca from the unjust silence which muffled his work, both within Spain and internationally, until the mid-1970's.[3] That Lorca's life and work should have become such a powerful source of inspiration for both artist and critic alike is of course a huge accolade in itself to the imaginative scope of his world. But not infrequently academic critics try to separate Lorca's work from the colourful aura of the person who produced it and to draw it out from under the pall of Civil War martyrdom, claiming that superficial issues of personality and biography only serve to simplify and to distort an artistic project which transcends them both. A typical and balanced statement of this view is that of Nicholas Round:

Often associated with the poeta maldito *[doomed poet] motif are epithets like 'dionysiac', 'demonic', or 'telluric'. These displace the inapt image of Lorca the happy folklorist, only to supplant it with folklore of another kind, playing down the consciously modern input of craft and culture which so largely shaped his creative process. Here it is not the nineteenth-century reference [of conventionally Romantic views of the poet] which misleads, but the easy assertion of a timeless spontaneity. As with other encapsulations of Lorca, a natural desire for simplicity is flattered; understanding of the more complex reality risks being lost.*[4]

Clearly, all things being equal, this call for dispassion, the desire to let the work speak for itself, has much to recommend it. But there is a very potent feeling in some Lorca circles that all things are not equal, at least not yet. While there is general agreement that those issues external to Lorca's writings – his imposing personality, the swirl of admirers who surrounded him, his flamenco caché, the circumstances of his murder – should be seen as no more than accoutrements to a body of work which stands amongst the most original of the twentieth century. There are also many who are worried that the facts and, more importantly, the determining influence of Lorca's homosexuality have been relegated to this list of peripherals.

Silence and Absences

The central concern of this book is the extent to which Lorca's work is the inevitable expression of his sexual dissidence, most explicitly perhaps in terms of his respect for cultural and sexual difference, his celebration of alternative ways of being in a time and place of deeply rooted intransigence. Lorca's sexual non-conformity was the source of his radical critique of society and its power relations. But the prehistory of this book concerns the wall of silence which has been constructed around Lorca's homosexuality, the result of either explicit denial or the dismissive view which holds that his sexuality is just another streak of colour in the boldly painted flamenco legend. Of

Duende.

A BANQUET HELD IN 1936 IN HONOUR OF THE POET LUIS CERNUDA (SEATED AT THE HEAD OF THE TABLE). VINCENTE ALEIXANDRE AND LORCA ARE FIRST AND SECOND FROM THE LEFT, STANDING. THE CHILEAN POET PABLO NERUDA IS FIFTH FROM THE LEFT, ALSO STANDING

course, Lorca himself was particularly careful not to leave much written testimony of his intimate world. He frequented several gay coteries, mostly in Granada and Madrid, one of them at Vicente Aleixandre's house, but even those who knew him in these more relaxed environments have been singularly discreet in their public statements. Aleixandre's poetic portrait of his friend certainly gives a clear but still necessarily codified view of the suffering that the publicly unconfessable nature of his love caused him. Moreover, while the primary reasons for the poet's execution were political and anti-intellectual, there can be no doubt that his 'dubious sexuality', in the words of one contemporary newspaper account, was an additional factor; the justification of a brutalization that went beyond the call of fascist duty.[5] In 1977 the Spanish essayist Andrés Sorel interviewed one of the Falangist soldiers who was with Lorca during his final hours:

> *Of course they tortured him, especially up his ass. They called him a queer and beat him there. Afterwards he could hardly walk.*[6]

Gibson adds more unpalatable details in his *The Death of Lorca*. He relates the open boasting of one of Lorca's killers in a packed bar in Granada:

> *[Juan Luis] Trescastro swaggered in and exclaimed for everyone to hear: 'We have just killed Federico García Lorca. We left him in a ditch and I fired two bullets into his arse for being a queer.'*[7]

That is why the subsequent programme of denial to which Lorca's sexuality has been subject not only devalues our attempt to understand his work in terms of its full range of meanings, but is also the posthumous continuation of the same injust silence he felt constrained to live under throughout his entire life. As the Spanish novelist, the Andalusian Antonio Muñoz Molina, aptly put it in a newspaper article in 1998, any reconstruction of Lorca which displaces or denies his sexuality also denies him the reality of his life and of his death.

While Lorca's sexuality is now recognized as a defining factor of his life and work, there have been and continue to be serious efforts either to ignore or to underplay it, or to dismiss it as part of a colourful and essentially folkloric representation. In 1962, for example, Fernando Vázquez Ocaña, who had known Lorca personally, was able to write that Federico 'never clouded his song with the unconfessable cries of the flesh'. He later referred to envy as the primary reason why lesser beings tend to attribute 'Wildean tendencies to men of greatness'.[8] And, dipping virtually at random into the same pool of denial, from a book published in 1980 we read the following account from Cristina Gómez Contreras, with whose family Federico maintained a friendly relationship:

> *When he was alive, we never heard the slightest whisper against him. And*
> *certainly not that he was an invert [...] If there had been anything strange about*
> *him, [my husband and brother-in-law] would have realised pretty quickly and they*
> *would have shown him the door, and prevented their women and children and*
> *families from having any further dealings with him. There's no truth to any of this.*
> *It's been made up by people who were jealous of him or who have nothing better*
> *to do with their time.*[9]

One of the abiding images of Lorca's work is that of the scream of humanity
raging in the face of an imposed wall of order and silence. It is savagely ironic
that silence and secrecy have surrounded much of the man's life and work,
even in death.

Sex in Sombre Times

The cultural perception of homosexuality in Spain is clearly central to all of
this. One of the great issues of Spanish culture is the tension between law and
the social codes on one hand, and the destructive force of desire on the other.
Whether seen as a personal trauma or an issue of public concern, Spanish
dramatists and poets have returned obsessively to this tension. Throughout
much of Spanish history, when officially sanctioned codes of conduct have
been built upon the bedrock of a traditional Catholic mentality, sexuality
fulfilled was either, depending upon one's point of view, a sin or a miracle.
And around sex, as around all sins and miracles throughout human history,
grew up a cult which, in its moment, Francoist theatre and cinema reflected
as faithfully as the unwelcome attentions of the censor's sluggish blue pencil
would allow. In the hunger that this cult of sex expresses one can detect clear
overtones of a yearning for a qualitatively different way of being. The Spanish
people as Adela in the national house of Alba, so to speak. And equally
clearly, the very liberal attitude towards things sexual which has characterized
Spanish public life since the death of General Franco is rooted in this

experience of a culture in which enforced chastity was perceived as being a function – the most intensely personal – of an undemocratic political system.

One of Lorca's major achievements was to dramatize sex as a fundamental subversion of the established order of things. The deepest roots of this project lie in his homosexuality, but when Lorca was 'rediscovered' in the times of transition between dictatorship and democracy, his more overtly homosexual pieces – most notably *The Public*, not performed until the mid-1980s, and *The Sonnets of Dark Love* – remained under official wraps. The effect of this was that Lorca's best-known works – *Blood Wedding, Yerma* and *The House of Bernarda Alba* – were eagerly consumed by the newly democratic and generally youthful audiences as powerful commentaries on the oppression of women in particular and on sexuality as a metaphor for freedom in general. In this way, of course, Lorca's theatre caught the mood of the times. And even better, he was one of the victims of the previous regime in the most direct and brutal sense. A poet of the sacrifice.

So Lorca's name became synonymous with the cause of a personal freedom stirringly – and meaningfully – expressed through the imagery of sexual liberation; but while most of Spain seemed to accept heterosexual freedom as part and parcel of the nation's new democratic project, attitudes towards homosexuality seemed slower in the changing, especially amongst those whose views had been cut during the *ancien régime*. Put simply, while pronounced heterosexual activity was politically *de rigueur*, gay was a personal matter, to be embraced, accepted or rejected as one's moral code, biological programming, or testosterone dictated. The upshot of this is that there are those today in Spain and abroad who still find it possible to profess love for Lorca's work while refusing to accept that his status as a gay man is an integral and inseparable element of his art.

Whatever the reasons underlying the construction of the official version of Lorca's image (a version, it should be noted, which right up until 1986 also coloured the only authorized translations of the works), the impact it has had on the dissemination of his work has been extraordinarily negative. Two extreme examples concern the belated publication of two of Lorca's most openly gay works, the play *The Public* (which Lorca actually described as 'frankly homosexual'; this is the sole occasion on which there is any record of him having used the word) and the suite of poems *Sonnets of Dark Love*. An initial version of the former appeared virtually as an extended quotation in a book by Rafael Martínez Nadal, whose English-language translation was published in London in 1974.[10] As a result, it is only in the last ten years or so that this play has received premieres in Spanish, French and English. Lorca's own description of the piece as a 'play to be booed at' is of course a statement of his own unease that the 'frankly homosexual' subject matter of the play would yield considerable evidence to the powerful forces ranged against him. But it also speaks of the creative arrogance of a truly master playwright who knows instinctively that his work will only achieve its real impact and meaning in times to come. The case of the *Sonnets of Dark Love* is even more curious.[11] Their belated appearance in a 19-page clandestine edition printed in and distributed free of charge from Granada in 1983 seemed to take the Lorca Estate wholly by surprise. The publication, instantly denigrated as 'pirated' by the Estate, was hailed by writers and critics alike. The by-then octogenarian Vicente Aleixande, for example, who had first mentioned this missing manuscript by name as far back as 1937, hailed the unqualified importance of what the poems' anonymous editor had done. Meanwhile the Estate responded by publishing the full suite of 11 poems in a national newspaper, *ABC*, a curious choice given the right-wing monarchist views which this particular paper openly espouses. And very quickly a group of distinguished scholars rallied round to declare that the 'dark love' of the title was not Lorca's version of the love that dares not tell its name, but a transcendental reference to love in many guises – universal, secret, despairing – but not necessarily homosexual. However, despite this, the commonly held interpretation of the title remains that these poems are outpourings of homosexual love. An interpretation reinforced by the fact that Lorca himself compared them to Shakespeare's sonnets at a time when the Bard's own sexuality was being hotly debated.

Bearing in mind that Federico García Lorca is one of the century's great artists, the fact that we cannot be sure whether there are significant writings still to come is astonishing. Certainly, a number of major works have been released in recent years, including the powerful *Play Without a Title*. But there are huge gaps in his imperfectly published *Complete Works*. Among them is his correspondence with the also homosexual Vicente Aleixandre, which would surely have cast some light into the heart of Lorca's intimate world. In the Catalogue to the centenary exhibition in Madrid's Reina Sofía Museum, Ian Gibson raises one of the few dissident voices among the rather more neutral scholars assembled there. In his brief 'Lorquian Absences' he sums up, cogently and directly, with Orwellian clarity, what I have described as this book's prehistory:

> *Of course we should seek to know everything, absolutely everything, about this unique being who with his work has enriched and continues to enrich the humanity of millions of people round the world. But in spite of the great gathering of information about the poet and his circumstances, sadly there are still innumerable gaps. Firstly, even though Lorca's homosexuality is referred to much more openly today and critics now take it into account in their assessments of his work, the silence which for decades shrouded this aspect of the poet's personality has meant that numerous testimonies which could have been crucial to our full understanding of this man have, simply, been lost.*[12]

There then follows a sad and frustrating litany of unpublished correspondence and withheld private papers — the correspondence with Aleixandre already mentioned, letters from several of Lorca's known lovers, among them the sculptor Emilio Ladrén and the man who also worked as his personal secretary, Rafael Rodríguez Rapún, intimate papers in the possession of Rafael Martínez Nadal which seem to hint at other affairs (there is a coyly truncated mention in one of a *torerillo* [a young bullfighter] whom Lorca had just met in Granada), a huge portion of the potentially explosive correspondence with Salvador Dalí and, most touchingly of all perhaps, the writer's correspondence with his mother (of whom more later).

Denial in Democratic Times

This tension between the two Federicos, one the consummate artist whose work apparently transcends the reality of the flesh, the other the homosexual martyr, boiled over in the summer of 1998 as both sides took up opposing positions in the centenary celebrations. An acrimonious debate was sparked off by Lorca's nephew and director of the Lorca Foundation, Manuel Fernández Montesinos. He declared in Granada that his uncle's literary status would be best served if the colourful panoply of Andalusian, political and homosexual trappings could be ignored in favour of close scrutiny of his actual ideas and writings.[13] Things were made worse when Spain's most recent Nobel laureate, novelist Camilo José Cela, came clambering into the debate by writing in *El País* of his unremitting hostility to the presence of groups of gay men in the celebrations, and declaring that when his own time for such honours came he would prefer 'a more solid, less anecdotal' commemoration on the basis that he himself 'had never been buggered'.

A caustic response was not long in coming. The gay Catalan novelist Terenci Moix, also writing in *El País*, took Cela to task. He not only expressed his total lack of surprise at the fact that Cela's bottom should have inspired such a paucity of amorous attention, but more seriously, by drawing attention to Cela's own dubious past (in the early 1940's he had volunteered his services as a spy and censor to the new Francoist regime), he established an explicit linkage between homophobic intransigence and the traditional Spain which had, in its time, claimed Lorca's life. Others were quick to join the offensive, with many objecting to the fact that the expensively mounted centenary exhibition in Madrid's Reina Sofía Museum, supported by the Lorca Foundation, seemed virtually to ignore both the dreadful circumstances of Lorca's murder and his homosexuality. My own impression when I visited the exhibition in July 1998 was that such complaints were indeed well founded. There were very few, if any, references to Lorca's homosexuality in the entire suite of rooms dedicated to his life and work (apart from the Gibson disclaimer in the Catalogue, which was quoted above). Moreover, although many people were expressing their repugnance at the fact that the right-wing Prime Minister José María Aznar was claiming on Lorca's birthday that 'today we are all Federico', the exhibition studiously avoided any specific reference to the political circumstances which led to the poet's death. Instead, a faded copy of the death certificate, which insultingly confirmed that the demise of Federico García Lorca was as a result of 'wounds sustained in acts of war', was pinned to an archway at the other side of which was a wall-sized image of a jubilant Federico in apparent celebration of his elevation to eternal glory. Of course, that is the way we would all wish to remember him. But Lorca's life, his work and letters, are riddled with the silences and veiled allusions which are part and parcel of his developing relationship with his own homosexuality. To recognize those silences and to clarify the allusions is to understand fully the sexual dissidence of a writer whose work prefigures the great sexual revolution of this century. But to take the absences for granted, to impose new layers of silence on top of them, is to collaborate with that uniform and oppressive culture.

Where Federico García Lorca is concerned, emotions run high. Lorca's homosexuality, whether acknowledged or disavowed, still sits astride a major fault line in Spanish culture. Homosexuality is of course more tolerated than before, but there is still something of a sideshow feel to it. If the radical cultural perceptions that spring from the homosexual artist's sense of difference are applied to the deepening of our understanding of the relationship between men and women, this is much less welcome. Of course, Lorca was more than painfully aware of this himself. In *Yerma*, for example, the brutish husband takes the rap for five centuries of Spanish *machismo*. An act of symbolic vengeance for which the traditional Spanish right was not to forgive Lorca. That is what this book is about. It will certainly not suggest that Lorca's work is intelligible only in terms of a homosexual reading. But it will argue that Lorca's sexuality, and above all the crisis of being homosexual in a society that gifted the word *macho* to the world, is a key to the very distinctive sense of life that informs his work. To ignore Lorca's sexuality or to minimize the implications of that crisis is to devalue the man and to misunderstand his achievement.

The Fall From Grace

The Sweet Times

Although Lorca usually claimed that he was born with the century, the year of his birth was 1898. In every sense though this is a more crucial date for the development of Spanish modernity than the mere symbolism of the century's turning. For it was in 1898 that an inglorious struggle with that *arriviste* on the world stage, the United States, led to the loss of Cuba and the Philipines, the last-remaining colonies in the glorious dream of Spanish empire. The event was to have notable consequences for the cultural and intellectual life of the country. A sense of historical displacement of the sort that Britain defused with the Falklands War (the national trauma that would have resulted from defeat in the South Atlantic is not hard to imagine) and of increasing social fragmentation led an entire generation of thinkers and writers to reflect long and hard upon the whole problematic business of being Spanish. In cultural terms at least, it was a time of deep national introspection. But although the work of the writers who came to be called the Generation of '98 is still of some relevance in the Spain of today, to the outsider much of it seems exclusively absorbed in its scrutiny of the national navel.[1] The problem, perhaps, is that few of its members were able to reflect their sense of national trauma through the more universal language of personal crisis – Unamuno, Machado and Valle-Inclán are notable and worthy exceptions. This is in contrast, for example, to the way that the great Irish writers of this century have memorably reflected the fault lines of their history and the dislocations of their society through the foibles and failings of characters of universal scope. It really fell to the coming generation of writers, of which the young Federico García Lorca was part, to diagnose the condition of their time and place in a body of work whose range of meanings and impact are genuinely universal. For more than most, Lorca was to experience the business of being Spanish as a deeply intimate problem.

FEDERICO GARCÍA LORCA, AGED 6

News of the loss of the colonies would certainly have been a major talking point in Fuentevaqueros, in the province of Granada, where Federico was born. But it is hard to imagine that the sense of national trauma would have done anything other than cause a ripple on the surface of a booming rural economy. Moreover, the loss of Cuba to the United States brought about a new demand for Spanish-produced sugar. And thanks to the business acumen of the future poet's father, who had wisely turned his lands on the rich plain of La Vega, just outside the city of Granada, to the cultivation of sugar-beet, the young Federico was born into comparative affluence. But of course the shock-waves caused by the sense of national shame were to exercise a profound long-term affect on all aspects of life. As the country turned increasingly inwards, the tension between traditionalist and modernizing (generally liberal and leftist) elements became more pronounced. The so-called 'Two Spains', the convenient short-hand description for the history of a nation internally riven, were already drawing their lines for the fratricidal conflict which would explode in 1936. The great poet Antonio Machado penned the following when Federico was still an adolescent:

> Little spanish child, born
> To the world today, may God
> In his mercy be kind
> For one of our two Spains
> Will freeze your heart
> To its deepest core.[2]

This view of the child's heart frozen through the experience of life in a country torn between diametrically opposed ways of being could very easily have been drawn from Lorca's work, indeed from his most intense personal experience. Much of his mature work provides versions on the theme of the human heart struggling against the numbing reality of an oppressive patriarchy. And in doing so, he was to draw upon himself the wrath of one of these two Spains, the all-powerful world of traditional Catholicism.

There was of course very little in Lorca's childhood world which suggested the radically subversive literature he was later to create. Federico was the first of four children, and rapidly developed the rich imaginative world which seems to be so frequently associated with the first-born of the family. He was able to develop his early passion for music, thanks largely to the talents of his mother, Vicenta Lorca Romero, and it was this together with her love of literature (she would read favourite pieces out loud to the servants) which prompted the adult Lorca to declare that everything he was and everything he would be, he owed to his mother.[3] This, however, did not prevent him from speculating in front of fading photographs about the woman 'who could have been my mother', Matilde Palacios, his father's first wife who had died four years before his birth. The great strength of Lorca's work, his imaginative identification with what might have been or might be in the face of what resolutely is, was already becoming apparent. He lived with one mother, but was haunted by another.

Vicenta Lorca was a devout Catholic and Federico would trot dutifully along with her to Mass.[4] In 'My Village', one of his earliest pieces of prose writings, he describes his growing fascination with the ritual of the liturgy, a fascination which was later both to influence his love for the theatre and to transform itself loosely into the ritualistic elements of his drama – the final scene of *Blood Wedding* is a good example. But in the same piece of early writing he also notes how his growing aesthetic excitement is tempered by an already deeply ingrained sense of sin:

> *When the organ began to play, the incense to rise, and the tiny bells to ring, I would become so excited... and then grow terrified of sins which, today, no longer worry me.*[5]

What these sins may be, the young writer does not explicitly say. But it is clearly likely that they were associated with the first stirrings of sexuality. So while Federico's mother 'more than anyone else, had moulded his artistic temperament', as Gibson claims, it is also certainly true that the boy's sense of shame and guilt was also initially fired by his mother's staunch Catholicism.[6] Unable throughout his whole life to discuss his sexuality openly with her, Lorca's relationship with his mother was always to be both close and unbearably secretive. It is a tension that he explores and attempts to resolve in his art. Images abound both of the authoritarian mother who, in *The House of Bernarda Alba*, for example, derives from Lorca's inculcated guilt and self-loathing rather than an unmediated representation of his own mother, as well as of the tender maternal figure capable of all understanding and love. Such a mother in potential is Yerma, the childless eponymous heroine of the play written in 1933. Lorca had by this time learnt that Matilde Palacios, his father's first wife, had been declared barren, and one can only speculate on the extent to which Yerma's deep maternal qualities, tragically denied, are rooted in the young Federico's search for a more understanding and compassionate otherness in those sepia photographs in the family album.

In a Spain where at that time traditional values were still firmly embodied in a comprehensive set of social taboos and expectations, it is perhaps inevitable that Federico's subsequent relationship with his family should exhibit a regressive demand for approval. His adolescent unease as to his own sexuality, the deep-rooted and, at that stage, still inescapable feeling that he was hiding something that was openly and widely disapproved of, was to leave a long and bitter residue. Throughout his life as a professional writer, he continuously sends cards and letters to his family, telling them how successful he has been, how much money his plays are earning, how warm the reception he has received in places as exotic as New York, Santiago de Cuba, and Buenos Aires, and so on.[7] This apparent vainglory can all too easily be interpreted as the bohemian son stressing that the world of the arts is not as prodigal as his middle-class parents might have assumed, that their initial investment in his studies is now bearing opulent fruit. Taken in this light, such letters become irksome. But if we read them from the point of view of the sexually prodigal son shoring himself up in his parents' affections, perhaps even unconsciously, against that moment of truth, of unbearable confession, they gain a new and moving significance. More so in view of the posthumous maintenance of the shroud of silence which he himself in life had struggled so painfully to hold in place.

The Bitter Times

Federico was six when the photograph reproduced on page 24 was taken. Well dressed, in an ornate setting, he is quite clearly a child of the comfortable middle classes. But in spite of this economic and social affluence, he enjoyed regular contact with people from all walks of life, from the maids in the family home, with their earthy exuberance, to local peasant children. He regularly herded all of them together as captive audiences for performances in which he would invariably play the role of priest or puppeteer. But more importantly he developed through them a deep love for the popular traditions, speech patterns and music of his native Andalusia. He quickly began to develop a spirited identification with the fertile countryside that surrounded his home. In an interview published in 1934, he talks with great nostalgia of his childhood sense of a nature that is animate and inhabited:

> This is the first time I've ever spoken about this... something so intimate and private that I've never wanted to analyse it. When I was a child I lived in the very heart of nature. And like all children I attributed to each single thing its own personality, each piece of furniture, each tree, each stone. There were some poplars at the back of my house. And one afternoon I realised that they were singing. The wind, as it passed between their branches, produced an arrangement of notes and tones that I thought of as music. And I would spend long hours singing along with the poplars... One day I stopped in amazement. Someone was saying my name, separating the syllables as though spelling it out: 'Fe...de...ri...co'. I looked around but no one was there. And yet I could still hear the whisper of my name... and I

listened and I listened until I found the source. It was the branches of an old poplar which, as they moved together, produced a monotonous whingeing tone, which seemed for all the world to be my name.[8]

From this one can begin to sense the magnetic power that, by all accounts, Lorca exerted over every social gathering. Equally, we can see how he is to some extent himself the architect of the popular image of the inspired poet of nature. But there is more to this than meets the eye. Nature is always present in Lorca's work as a life-force baulked by convention and social codes. But it is also there in all its glory, its vitality, through the horses, bulls and other animals, the flowers and the crops, the rivers, the mountains, the sea, the sky and the land, which the poet weaves into the characteristic imagery of his poems and plays alike. Nature, wild, harsh and rampant, rather than our more domesticated variety, gives Lorca's work both its backdrop and its deepest meaning.

Later in the same interview he gives another insight into his experience on the land, without which, he relates, he could not have written *Blood Wedding*:

It was about 1906. Where I'm from was farming land, and it had always been ploughed by old wooden ploughs which barely scratched the surface. But that year some of the farmers had got hold one of the new Bravant ploughs – I've never forgotten the name – which had won all sorts of prizes at the Paris Exhibition of 1900. My curiosity made me follow behind it. I loved watching how the huge steel share carved into the earth, drawing out branches instead of blood. One time the plough stopped. It had come to rest against something solid. A second later, that shining steel blade pulled up a Roman mosaic from the earth. There was an inscription, which I've forgotten now, although it could very well have been to do with Daphnis and Chloe. So my first sense of artistic wonder is linked to the earth [...] My first emotions are linked to the earth and the working of the fields. Which is why I have what psychoanalysts would call an 'agrarian complex'.[9]

This is a more telling anecdote, indicating an art rooted in a sense of earth, whose central concern is to uncover the buried bonds between humankind and the clay from which we have sprung. So it is that in the climactic scene of *Blood Wedding*, when the runaway Leonardo and the Bride are struggling not solely to justify their violent elopement – the force of nature flowing within them is communicated as a destiny beyond motivation – but specifically to find a language of exculpation from the powerful sense of sin with which they have grown up, Lorca uses the image of earth to suggest the powerful compulsion motivating what may otherwise be seen as simple sexual choice:

> Leonardo: It's not my fault;
> It's the earth that's to blame;
> It's the scent of your breasts
> And of your hair.[10]

In other words, all of those who respond to the sensuous voice of their nature will one day need to find an answer to the ingrained questioning of sin and blame. It was, after all, an issue which had preoccupied Federico throughout his own adolescent years. And if we read between the lines of Aleixandre's cautious depiction of a Lorca whose moments of private darkness were inspired by his closeted love, then it seems that in many ways it was an issue which stayed with him throughout his short adult life as well.

So land and the sense of the land give Lorca's work both its central arena of action and its obsessive themes. By talking with those who worked in the fields or by simply observing their rhythm of productivity, Federico was irresistibly drawn into the continual struggle to produce life in the midst of harsh desolation, towards the relief inspired in the oasis of fertility which was La Vega, where greenery no sooner bursts into life than it is consumed under the burning sun. It is not hard to see from this why green becomes the primary colour in the palette of a writer whose extraordinary sensitivity to colour and strongly visual imagination were born in the heightened perceptions of the play of light on land. Nor is it difficult to understand why green for Lorca signals both life's intensity and its fragility, that all too fleeting moment of blossom before the inevitability of rapid decay. It may be, too, that the vaguely tragic sense that Lorca describes as having beset him since childhood has its origins as much in the young boy's experience of the rhythms of the land as it does in a fearful sense of sin. In the lecture which he wrote to accompany public readings of *Gypsy Ballads* (his first commercially successful book of poetry, published in 1928), he describes another 'possible', but crucial, childhood memory:

> *I was eight years old and playing at home in Fuentevaqueros when another boy suddenly looked in through the window. He was like a giant, and he glared at me with a scorn and hatred that I shall never forget. Just as he moved to go, he spat at me, and I heard a distant voice calling 'Amargo, come on! Come on, Amargo!'.*
>
> *After that, this Amargo grew inside me until at last I understood why he had looked at me like that – for he is the angel of death and of despair that guards the doors of Andalusia. The figure has become an obsession in my poetic work.*[11]

The name 'Amargo' means 'bitter one', and Lorca was later to write a number of poems in which he presents the 'bitter one' as one of the key figures of his work. There the figure is characterized by both his swaggering embrace of life and an unswerving instinct for death, so that he comes to stand in Lorca's mind for the complex of emotions inspired by the simultaneous contemplation of life's intensity and its fragility.

For the young Federico, death became a constant and daunting companion, a natural and integral part of everyday life on the land. We can perhaps understand the appearance of the 'Amargo' to the young Federico, as Paul Binding suggests, in terms of the sudden burgeoning of this 'peasant' reality in the boy's hitherto cosseted bourgeois existence.[12] Lorca's subsequent artistic endeavour is a way of keeping death at bay, not by ignoring it, but by calling it and playing it as the bullfighter plays the bull. The images of death, and especially of violent death, which recur constantly in Lorca's work, therefore, are rarely gratuitous. They are a counterpoint to life itself, in their own way a celebration of vitalism, of the only life worth living – a life of brilliance in an infinity of darkness. There may well be some sense of that 'black and baleful Spanish obsession with death' in Lorca, as the Scottish writer Hamish Henderson has claimed.[13] But it is a vision of darkness which does not negate life; rather it highlights it, always geared as it is towards that intensification of experience that springs from the conscious realization that our days are numbered. It is precisely this dangerous but exhilarating challenge to a death foretold which is ritualized in the bullfight. And that is why, just a few months before he was to meet his own violent end in a way which suggested another death foretold, Lorca was to declare that the bullfight 'is the most cultured festival in the world today [...] the source of our greatest poetry and vitality'.[14] During his so-called student years in Madrid, he developed his own death-defying ritual, playing dead in front of his friends, initially enjoying their concern, and subsequently their mock grief. The common interpretation is that in this way Federico exorcised his fear of death. But always fearful of being the object of gossip, he would also have been reassured by the apparently objective tones of their funeral eulogies. His secrets had died with him.

The adolescent's burden of sinful thoughts and unconfessable desires, and his growing awareness of death shatter the magic sensation of connectedness that Lorca describes as characterizing his relationship with the external world. He is impure and unbearably alone – another way, perhaps, of understanding the Amargo story. He hides his sexuality from his parents, concealing what he had been taught to think of as the hidden seams of shame and guilt from everyone who knows him. But people do suspect. His schoolmates are already beginning to call him Federica and refuse to play with him.[15] Sin, with its wages of death, formed the common denominator of life for virtually every sexually aware youngster in Spain (indeed, incomparably more so, if that growing sexuality produced doubly illicit passions). If any of them had met and compared notes with their Irish counterparts (as Lorca inevitably did when he first read J M Synge), they would have found they had a great deal in common.[16] And when three young Spanish men, all from broadly similar backgrounds, all similarly sensitive to the abyss between their own needs and the death-peddling imagery of religious negation, were eventually to meet in Madrid in the 1920s, they inevitably discovered a deeply shared inheritance. They were of course Federico García Lorca, Salvador Dalí and Luis Buñuel. But before meeting them, to share in their anger, fear and rebellion, Federico still had a lot of his own ground to travel.

Singing the Bitterness

It was thanks to the specifically Spanish preoccupations of the Generation of '98 that Federico published his first book, discovering in the process that, amongst all his extraordinary battery of skills and talents, his literary vocation was probably the most viable. The interest of writers like Unamuno and Machado in the Spanish landscape, and their search there for a bedrock of values upon which to begin to identify and characterize Spanish identity, had led to a proliferation of travel books. Suitably inspired, one of Lorca's university teachers, Martín Domínguez Berrueta, took a number of his charges, including the avid Federico, on two study visits, firstly through Andalusia, then northwards into the heartland of Castile, and finally to the Celtic fringe of Galicia. The year was 1916, and Federico had just embarked upon the twin study of Law and Letters in the University of Granada; Berrueta's excursions not only seemed of enormous cultural relevance to the nascent, restless artist, they also offered the opportunity of pure escape to the disaffected student. Lorca immersed himself in the unchanging elements of the Spanish cultural landscape, whether he was recording the timeless Spanish image of the old woman in black shuffling past the fountain in a whitewashed village square, or meeting with some of the acknowledged literary giants of the day, like Unamuno and Machado. Later he worked through his notes from

the journeys and added some more of his reflections and impressionistic portraits of the gardens, churches, villages, customs and landscapes of a Spain that in many ways exists even today, surviving the tremendous changes of the transition to democracy and the post-modernization of the economy. The result was *Impressions and Landscapes*. His first book, and he had barely turned twenty.

It is a typical first work in many respects, in one way, derivative, in another, a testing ground for new ideas. Derivative in that it is permeated with a ninety-eightist melancholy (which the non-specialist reader might easily – and legitimately – take for a late-flowering, bucolic sort of romanticism), but also innovative in that the poet's eye for the genuinely illuminating detail gives the book an air of voluptuous and languid pleasure that is unmistakably Lorquian. Here is just one tiny example, taken from the brief section entitled 'Noon in August':

> *In all the immense landscape the only sound is that of the cicada, drunk on light and song.*
> *Noon. The gentle breeze picks through shimmering patterns of heat. Beyond the immense blast of naked heat over the fields stand the green-black lines of the poplar groves. The fields are deserted. The labourers are asleep in their houses...*
> *A field of poppies is slowly dessicating. The great symphony of light dazzles and blinds the eye.*
> *Amidst this silence and peace, the curfew sounded, charged and voluptuous... An interrogation of the flesh...*
> *The women from the village are bathing in the river, shrieking with pleasure as the cool water licks around their naked bellies and breasts. The village lads, like fauns, spy on them from the undergrowth. All of nature becomes a giant copulation, rearing up on desire. Bees drone monotonously. And the boys roll amongst the flowers and the bushes as they watch a young girl come naked from the water, her breasts high, wringing her long hair dry as the others playfully splash her belly with water...*
> *The quail in the wheatfield begins to sing.*[17]

It is clear from the poems that he was writing around this time that Lorca had recognized the nature of his own sexual drive. But given the literary models that he had to follow, as well as the social and family pressures that he so keenly felt, we shouldn't wonder why he should have fixed on what to all intents and purposes is a highly charged heterosexual scene. But it is not entirely a question of dissimulation. On one level, he is clearly attempting to recover through the scene his lost sense of connectedness. For this is not writing which merely depicts, like a Poussin canvas, a scene of bucolic eroticism; it is a deeply felt evocation of the erotic principle which underpins all of creation. Above all, we see here one of his great abilities: the fixing of emotion in and through very real elements of the natural world. It is a world which remains animate; but now it is inhabited by the sexual energy that Federico was experiencing within himself as a source of profound difference. At this stage, he can be little more than the observer of this heterosexual microcosm, an outsider singing its ritual, physically apart, but at least still connected through his own sexual charge to a more profound erotic principle. Like the tiny quail singing, lost in the midst of nature's splendour. But perhaps not fully understanding it ... yet.[18]

Much more directly personal was his first volume of poetry, *Book of Poems*, published in 1921.[19] The 68 poems are individually dated, so that we know that the final composition of the book took place between the spring of 1918 and late summer of 1920, although early versions of some were written when the poet was as young as sixteen. The author's 'Words of Justification' prepares the reader not just for a work of confession – 'the youthful ardour and torture, the measureless ambition, the exact image of the days of my adolescence and youth' – but one in which the writer is already seeking an escape from the pain of that confession – 'Above all of its errors, above its sure and certain limitations, this book has the virtue, among others I think, of reminding me throughout of the impassioned child that I was, running naked through river meadows with the mountains rising high behind'. Once again an attempt to rebuild the shattered connectedness. The highly condensed form of these lyrical poems and their ability to evoke the profoundest emotional states through a cohesive and systematic 'grammar of imagery' (the phrase is Stephen Spender's) drawn from the observation of everyday Andalusian life, give the collection its unmistakable voice.[20] Lorca will subsequently explore a dazzling range of forms and media, but this precocious *Book of Poems* presents us with an artist whose central themes are already established. Using the negative language of doubt, anguish, self-questioning, these central themes of sex and death are explored with a passionate intensity which allows many poems of this collection to soar far above the stock romantic melancholy which provides the background wash to its occasionally lurid splashes of adolescent colour.

Above all else, the book is permeated by a profound sense of loss as the poet contemplates his distant childhood and the fall from grace which early manhood entails, the tumbling into an awareness of death and sexual difference, and the bridge of sin and guilt which joins them both. Federico is again the marginalized observer, watching the codes of the heterosexual world as they play themselves out in the time-honoured rituals from which he is now excluded. From 'Song in a Minor Key', written when he was twenty:

> Girls in gardens
> Say goodbye
> As I pass them by. the bells
> Ring me out goodbye.
> And the trees kiss
> In the evening air as
> I weep along the street,
> Grotesque and without solution,
> Burdened with the grief of Cyrano
> And Don Quijote...

This is not one of the best poems in an uneven collection. Nevertheless, it provides a good window into the state of mind of a young man obsessed with what might have been, with the lost world of marriage and procreation (expressed through the clichéd image of the bells). Federico had not yet honed his radical edge, too inexperienced to turn his sense of being a sexual outsider into the questioning of social codes and institutions which was to inform much of his later work; on the other hand, the fact that he felt himself condemned to childlessness was to be a permanent source of sorrow, one which certainly contributed to the constant sense of the impossibility of things which pervades his work.

In another poem, 'Madrigal' (dated October 1920), the young man recalls an encounter, presumably heterosexual, that has gone sadly awry. In a letter to a friend dated around the same time, he confesses that he frequently resorts to a *macho* pose he finds repugnant:[21]

> My kiss was a pomegranate,
> Open and deep;
> Your kiss,
> A paper rose.

The proximity of the female body brings about a new ringing of the metaphorical bells, tolling once again not for joy but as a reminder of his exclusion from this community and its rites, tolling a farewell to his own childhood dreams. In this state of self-pity, all that is left is to lock himself into his stagnant destiny and watch the rest of the world go sexually by:

> Now, grave master,
> To the high schoolroom,
> To my love and my dreams
> (Eyeless horses all).

FEDERICO IN GRANADA, 1919

It seems that the wisdom born from suffering can be the only possible fruit of his sexual difference. But this suffering was to lead to an impassioned understanding of our deepest nature, an understanding which, in the fullness of time, developed into a coherent and constructive rupturing of traditional representations of male and female sexuality. But for the moment he feels locked into the despairing contemplation of his own frustration and sterility – the image of the 'eyeless horses' refigures Oedipus blinding himself for his unconfessable love at the same time as it prefigures the 'horse with the dagger in its eye' in *Blood Wedding*, an *Equus*-like evocation of the self-mutilation that guilt inflicts in the wake of illicit desire. As Federico suffers, the great writer is born.

The key moment in *Book of Poems*, however, the one which gives a glimpse of the subversive writer within the confused young man, occurs in 'If only my hands...'. The reference is to the children's game 'He loves me, he loves me not' as petals are torn one by one from a daisy. The poem, written when Lorca was twenty-one, is worth quoting in its entirety:

> I pronounce your name
> On those dark nights
> When stars come
> To drink in the moon,
> When black branches
> Sleep through hidden leaves.
> And I feel drained
> Of all passion and music.
> A crazed clock
> Singing out each and every
> Dead hour.
>
> I pronounce your name
> On this dark night
> And your name sounds

More distant than ever.
More distant than all the stars,
Sadder than the gentlest rain.

Will I love you again
As I loved you then? how can
My heart be held to blame?
And when the darkness lifts
What other passion awaits?
How serene, how pure?
If my fingers could pluck
The living petals from the moon!

The moment of rebellion, the anguished question 'How can my heart be held to blame' will echo and re-echo throughout the rest of Lorca's work. It is his first moment of acceptance, of himself and of all others like 'the boy who dresses as a bride/in the closet's darkness' just as much as 'the little boy/who writes a girl's name on his pillow', as he was later to write in his great 'Ode to Walt Whitman'. It is Federico's moment of Terentian wisdom, his deep-rooted and far-reaching realization that *nihil humani a me alienum puto* ('nothing human is foreign to me'). His mature work will become both a celebration of the heart that screams 'no' and an obsessive probing of everything in life that is heartless. It marks the beginning of the process of reconstruction of his lost world of connectedness. A process which, although never completed, builds throughout his life to the final half-assertive and half-pleading realization in the *Sonnets of Dark Love*, written in his final year of life, 'For I am love, for I am nature!'

A Musical Interlude

Both of Federico's parents believed in the benefits to be gleaned from a good education. Lorca's father, Federico García Rodríguez, was an old-fashioned liberal who held firm views on self-improvement, while his mother had been a school teacher up until her marriage in 1897. Federico, however, proved to be a lacklustre pupil, displaying a fetchingly tolerant boredom with most subjects that was to carry over into his university days. What was extraordinary about the young boy was his multifaceted creativity. He quickly developed a love of music, and spent long hours at the piano, which can still be seen today in the family's final home in Spain, now the Lorca House-Museum in Granada. Originally, he yearned above all else to be a musician, and there can be no doubt from the evidence of both contemporary accounts and the few recordings of his playing that are still in existence, that he was a talented and genuinely engaging performer.[22] He began to collect and write new arrangements for the folk songs and tunes of Andalusia. These were lively ballads that were the first cousins of the more demanding forms of flamenco and *cante jondo*, or 'deep song'. His growing familiarity with these musical forms was to play an increasingly important role in his artistic development, as we shall see. But for the moment they also nourished his literary imagination with their colourful and highly condensed imagery, his dramatic sense with their stirring tales of violent passion, and his cultural and historical awareness with their flavour of the lost civilization of Islam.

Let us stay with the last of these aspects for the moment. At its deepest level, Lorca's work in its entirety can be seen as the attempt to reconstruct Spanishness and through that to redefine the space that Western Judeo-Christian civilization concedes to the individual's primal impulses. That Lorca should experience majority culture with its moral imperative of 'civilized' conduct as a site of repression should not be surprising. The tools which enforce civilized conduct, the law and ethics, have always in their origins been primarily concerned to subdue and domesticate. Lorca independently comes to the same conclusion as does Freud in his far-reaching *Civilization and its Discontents*, namely that society disactivates the emotions that come marauding from within through a carefully constructed system of ethical and psychological checks and balances imposed from without. The key word is of course 'independently'. Although Lorca would later actually come to read Freud, it would be largely through his interest in surrealism. Moreover, while the Austrian psychoanalyst was primarily concerned, at least in his clinical work, to restore a measure of bourgeois serenity to the fevered deviant's brow, the Spanish poet's ultimate intention remained much more radical: the deconstruction of a civilization and the redefinition of the individual's right to be, not through the language of ethics or of the law, but in terms of a natural imperative.

Federico very quickly realized that this search, the fruit of intense personal experience, was also a living issue of Andalusian culture, and that music provided a unique window into it. For several hundred years, until well into the fifteenth century, the Arab province of Al-Andalus had undoubtedly been one of the most genuinely civilized parts of Europe. The so-called liberation of Granada by Ferdinand and Isabella, the Catholic Monarchs, in 1492, marked the final unification of Spain and the culmination of the fervent sense of mission which had galvanized the various Christian kingdoms in the Iberian Peninsula up until then. It is a date sacred to Spanish traditionalists – in fact, the rhetoric and iconography of the Catholic Monarchs was ably enlisted five centuries later to the cause of Francoism. For Lorca, it was a date which sounded the death-knell of a civilization whose acceptance and celebration of the sensuous in human experience had made it admirable and unique.

However, the continued cultural presence of *cante jondo*, or deep song, convinced Lorca that the sensuous delicacy and emotional intensity of a long-disappeared and wholly disavowed civilization had not been totally lost. Instead, it had been sublimated deep within the Andalusian consciousness, just as the marvellous Mosque of Córdoba had been overlaid by a Gothic fortress cathedral. Deep song (not simply flamenco, which is its eighteenth-century offspring) is one of the very first manifestations of song, its origins lying in the ancient musical systems of the Afghanistan/India area. In Lorca's own words, while flamenco is relatively modern, *cante jondo* 'is imbued with the mysterious colour of primeval ages'.[23] It is a song beyond the sense of words, an attempt, in its origins at least, by the human voice to re-create the movement and flight of bird song. In that respect, we can see it as a cultural version of that childhood sense of connectedness that had been shattered by the way that he saw himself in the mirror of his own very different civilization.

Lorca always insisted that the culture of Spain in general and of Andalusia in particular was especially open to emotional intensity at its deepest. The implication of the life-restoring question 'How can my heart be held to blame?' is that art should prompt its viewer or reader back to a pre-civilized, pre-socialized response. In one of his most revealing and suggestive lectures, 'Theory and Play of the *duende*', first delivered in Buenos Aires in 1933, Lorca attempted to define this dark presence in his art in terms of the *duende*. Meaning literally 'lord of the house', the *duende* has passed into Spanish folklore as a puckish figure capable of intervening for better and for worse in the life of ordinary mortals (two *duendes* make their appearance in this guise in Lorca's theatre in his short play *The Love of don Perlimplín for Belisa in the Garden*). Lorca, however, generally uses the word in a much more strictly Andalusian sense, one which is intrinsically linked to the tradition of deep song and flamenco. Here it refers to that mysterious, perhaps indefinable power in a singer or dancer which elevates technical prowess to the level of great art. It is difficult to discuss these things without appearing to attribute mystical qualities to performance art, but it is certainly true that Lorca had a profound belief in a sort of Dionysian lifeblood, which can transfigure singer and song when both performer and spectator connect through a circuit which bypasses the rational. In that sense, Lorca saw *duende* as the shiver of response produced in the listener or spectator by the projection of emotional intensity against the constant awareness of death's inevitability – a sort of poltergeist of the emotions. For Lorca the *duende*, this 'mysterious power that everyone feels but which no philosopher can explain', comes from the power to peel back layers of restraint so that the quick of our emotional being is laid bare. The *duende* reorientates the listener or spectator towards the deepest root of his or her being:

> So the duende *is a power and not an action, a struggle and not a thought. I have heard an old guitar maestro say that the duende is not in the throat, but that it surges up inside you right from the soles of the feet.*[24]

It is clear from this statement why British actors, whose training remains largely inspired in the techniques of Stanislavsky, should experience difficulties with the emotional pitch of Lorca's theatre.[25] This renewed suggestion that it is our physical contact with the earth – in the sense of our ability to respond naturally and fully to sensual experience – which unleashes the disturbing force of the *duende* within us, does not imply that Lorca's art is an emotional outpouring measured only by the limits of sheer inspiration. Lorca was a consummate artist, fully aware that his art, whether his poetry or theatre, was a scaffold upon which the performer would construct his or her performance, and that such a scaffold required in turn a careful and safe construction. There is a clear and artful relationship between Federico's early experience of connectedness ruptured and the frustrated desires and baulked energies of his characters. At the heart of Lorca's poetry and theatre is the struggle to return to the true soil of belonging, of belonging to oneself, of belonging to nature; it is an escape from rational consciousness, an escape which inevitably brings the escapee, like the archetypal lovers of *Blood Wedding*, into the ambit and sway of the human heart of darkness itself.

For Federico deep song encapsulated this link between emotional intensity and darkness, even death:

> *Throughout the ages Spain has been moved by the* duende, *for it is a land of ancient music and dance where the duende squeezes the lemons of dawn - a land of death. A land open to death [...] Everywhere else death is an end. Death comes, and the curtains are drawn. But not in Spain. In Spain they are opened. Many Spaniards live indoors until the day they die, and only then are they taken out into the sun. A dead man in Spain is more alive than anywhere else in the world. His profile wounds like the edge of a barber's*

razor [...] Throughout the country, everything finds its final metallic value in death.[26]
He very quickly produced a book of poetry, *Poem of Deep Song*, whose central purpose was to give open expression to this heart of darkness kept alive hitherto in popular song. The poems were probably written in late 1921, when Federico was collaborating with his friend the composer Manuel de Falla in the organization of a Festival of Deep Song, significantly to be held in the Alhambra, the magnificent Moorish palace which overlooks Granada. Nearly a decade was to pass, however, before the *Poem of Deep Song* was to see publication in its final form. As so often in Lorca's professional life, *duende* and the printed word seemed mutually incompatible.

These are very much poems for performance, works whose condensed lyricism and forceful imagery reveal Lorca's desire to expose his reader/listener to the liberating influence of the *duende*, the shivering force of emotion communicated by 'everything that has black sounds'. Lorca's emblematic use of language, the linguistic verve and poetic eye which link unsoundable human experience to emotive details of the physical world, is honed in these poems:

> *It is remarkable, almost beyond understanding, how in just three or four lines the anonymous popular poet can condense the most intense emotional moments in human life. There are songs where the lyric tremor rises to a point which is inaccessible to all but a few poets:*

> > The moon is cold
> > In its halo.
> > My love has died.[27]

Once again, the link in Lorca's mind between emotional intensity and death is striking. Through this evocation of the sensuous poetry of a lost civilization and this attempt to recoup or release a voice which speaks from the heart of human experience, Federico is both asserting a culture in which he is at home and lamenting the absence of genuine freedom in his own society 'coffin-narrow with prescription'.[28] Like his identification with Islamic Granada, this cult of defeat and loss is a way of simultaneously giving form to and sublimating his own very present pain.

Changing Faces

Federico's life and published letters — or at least those that have escaped from the oblivion or the secret archives to which it seems so many others have been consigned — are riddled with silences and deeply veiled allusions to secrets. In 1918 he wrote, in an unusually explicit letter to a trusted friend, that he was publicly adopting a posture 'that is not true to my heart' and later that 'I mock [me burlo de] my own passions'.[29] The necessarily oblique nature of poetic expression has allowed him in *Book of Poems* to explore riven experience and emotions in tension, but the sense of personal inauthenticity which is increasingly corroding his external relationships inevitably filters through into his art. A common motif of his drawings, where the naïve element deliberately understates their depth of psychological introspection, is the double-faced clown or harlequin (see page 24), the outsider who masks his intimate reality from the assembled onlookers.[30] As Lorca's fame grew, clearly this became more and more of a burden, so that when he was first firmly in the public eye, at the time of the huge commercial success of *Gypsy Ballads* in 1928, his sense of being untrue to himself had become well nigh unbearable. The pressure of his own fame, of the maintenance of his public face, was one of the factors which drove him to New York in 1929.[31] It was only in the New World that Lorca was able to have 'reconciled himself, once and for all, to his own sexual anomaly' (in the interesting choice of phrase of Christopher Maurer, a major Lorca scholar and editor of the 1990 Penguin edition of *Poet in New York*).[32] But in one of the early poems of the New York collection, 'Back from a Walk', Lorca's crisis of identity appears to be heightened by his sense of anonymity and dislocation in the imposing geometry of New York:

>Murdered by the sky.
>Between shapes moving towards the snake
>And shapes seeking glass.
>I'll let my hair grow long.

>The amputated tree that no longer sings,
>The child with her egg-white face.

>Tiny animals with broken heads,
>The ragged water of dry feet.

>Everything in its silent mute weariness,
>The butterfly drowned in the ink-well.

>Stumbling across my different face every day.
>Murdered by the sky!

In this place, where nature has suffered the catastrophic onslaught of a brutalizing civilization – cut-back trees with no birds singing in their branches, mass-produced, insipid children and domesticated animals – where the enhancing sense of life's wonderful fragility, the butterfly, has been swamped under the ink stains of modern life, Lorca's whole experience of self is reduced or distilled to that of being simply another victim. His own nature has been twisted by conformism beyond the point that it can be considered a natural thing, like water that is dry. In that sense, it is possible to see the line with which the poem opens and closes as Lorca grieving for his destiny as a homosexual (in the original Spanish, the word *cielo* can be either 'heaven' or 'sky') as well as lamenting the living death that this civilization inflicts. This is reinforced by the determination to 'let my hair grow long', which some have seen as the new resolve to cultivate a more rebellious and explicitly androgynous identity.[33] Rather than expressing a pre-hippy image of free-

ONE OF LORCA'S DRAWINGS DEPICTING THE DOUBLE-FACED CLOWN

wheeling youth and subversive sexuality, however, long hair is surely here an echo of the biblical image of mourning. It is one which also occurs in the *Gypsy Ballads* (for example in 'Ballad of the Black Sorrow') as the outward sign of implosion, a personality which cannot maintain itself intact in the face of, in this case, the huge tensions between the temptations of sin (the serpent) and the warnings of the simplistic but devastating moral codes (the glass) upon which civilization rests.

This is a crisis which remained acute for about 20 years, from when Federico was about twelve (to judge by the New York poem '1910: interlude') to at least 1929 or 1930. Indeed, whether or not he ever succeeded in putting it completely behind him is debatable. The living of life in its fullness becomes

inextricably associated with a bitter aftertaste. We have already seen that he
described the cultural force of deep song as the *duende* squeezing 'the lemons
of dawn', a form and impulse which are simultaneously creative and
destructive. Living may well be squeezed to the maximum, but the bitter cup
remains to be drunk. For Federico, self-fulfilment and disaster, passionate
outbreak and destruction, go hand in glove. Self-fulfilment requires sincerity
with oneself, but sincerity with oneself will inevitably lead to him being
driven out of the decent drawing rooms of the middle classes, with all the
shame and scandal that would without doubt ensue from such social
ostracization. It is small wonder, therefore, that Federico developed an
abiding detestation of the bourgeoisie, and began to re-invent himself in and
through a radically different cultural expression. In *Poem of Deep Song* he
dedicates a single poem to the singer Juan Breva, whose voice he describes in
terms similar to the *duende* as possessing the quality of a 'sunless sea and an
orange squeezed dry'. This is the essence of the deep song tradition, from
which Lorca saw his own work and cultural preoccupations arising and to
which he longed to make a lasting and significant contribution. But it also
captures both his own desire to drain life to the dregs and his inability to
evade the sense of tragedy which rises up in the wake of this vital urge. The
point of access into this imagery is undoubtedly through the emotional
resonance (what Lorca called the 'lyrical tremor') of the words. Both art and
life – in the sense of Bergson's *élan vital*, or urgent, passionate life – spring from
the compressing of experience, from savouring the sensuous intensity which,
for Federico, was the essential dimension of being human. But this sweetness is
thrown into sharp perspective by the brooding presence of the 'sunless sea', a
foreboding image of death. Life, the right to be, the freedom to be oneself, are
all inevitably constrained.

Through deep song, therefore, Lorca was able to find a wider cultural mirror
for his own artistic and existential preoccupations. He also discovered there
the mask of performance, the way in which the performer can be
simultaneously public and private. In the piece about the great singer Juan

Breva, he talks about his performance as 'sorrow itself singing behind a smile'. There can be no doubt that this is how Federico actually saw himself, and this corresponds to Vicente Aleixandre's description of his public performance as 'winged genius dispensing its grace', while all the time suffering terribly in private because of love. In its own way, of course, this was to lead to Lorca's mature reflections on the way in which performance can be constructed and manipulated to communicate the tremor of concealed emotions within. But in many of his dealings throughout his life, the mask of social performance was an essential tactic, not a dramatic strategy. It was how Federico survived, and it was the source of his sense of bad faith. Furthermore, it is not difficult to see that some of the constituent elements of the Lorca legend – his dazzling conversation, the rapidity of his inspiration, his flamenco verve – are careful constructs of a persona with which, in the first instance, he distracts attention from his own reality (just as in Aleixandre's poem 'The Waltz', which was admired by Federico, 'the gentlemen divert attention with their moustaches/from their backsides'). Later, however, he would turn these qualities into the stuff of great art. For that to happen, he had to get out of Granada and hone his performance. The challenging new stage would be found in Madrid, with Salvador Dalí and Luis Buñuel in the role of demanding and anything but uncritical spectators.

The Realm of Law

A Paradise Closed to Many

By the time he was twenty, Federico had developed a distinctly ambivalent view of his home city of Granada. On the one hand, he was proud of, and fascinated by, the rich cultural heritage of a city that had been a shining jewel in the crown of Al-Andalus. He loved the atmospheric Alhambra, which at that time was still visible from the new family home in the Huerta de San Vicente. He had numerous friends in Granada's ebullient café society, and together they planned and published literary magazines and held poetry competitions. Above all else, perhaps, he felt part of something larger than himself, of a cultural and historical context through which he could put his own sexuality and the solitude arising from it into perspective. Not long before his death, he spoke in often quoted words of the enriched understanding of humanity which this Granada, the Granada of the colonized and dispossessed, had given him:

> *Being born in Granada has helped me to understand and feel for all those who suffer persecution – the Gypsy, the Black, the Jew and the Moor, which all Granadinos carry inside themselves.*

In 1492 the victorious Christians had expelled the Jewish and Moorish populations from Granada. Those who remained, promising religious and cultural conversion to Christianity, were, like the gypsies, subjected to a programme of social and political apartheid. Deep song, in that way, grew up as the music of the dispossessed, speaking a language of loss and loneliness. It is no wonder that Lorca should have identified so closely with it. Indeed, as we have seen, in many ways he saw the fall of Granada and the subsequent colonization of its varied peoples as a sort of objective correlative for his own situation. It was for that reason that he always maintained a link with Granada, returning frequently not solely to see family or to look up old friends, but also to re-immerse himself in the ancient, by now barely visible, culture of the city.

But Lorca also experienced the place as a nest of small-minded bourgeois intolerance. He would have of course been painfully aware of the widespread attitude of those who, like Cristina Gómez Contreras, would have shown him the door in no uncertain terms had he given any indication of who or what he really was. He was as bitter in his condemnation of what Granada had become as he was fulsome in his praise for what it was. In 1936, not long before his death, he spoke of his abhorrence for post-fall Granada:

> [The fall of Granada to the Christians] was a disastrous event, no matter what they've taught us in school. An admirable civilisation, with its poetry, its astronomy, its architecture, and a sensitivity unique in the world − all was sacrificed to the impoverished, cowed city of today, a paradise for the small-minded, the worst bourgeoisie in Spain...[1]

Clearly, these were not words geared towards endearing the poet to the more traditional and increasingly resentful sectors of Granada society. Moreover, Lorca had frequently referred to Granada's physical setting, hemmed in as it is at the foot of the massive Sierra Nevada, as a metaphor for its enclosed and stagnant nature. This was a view he had already begun to develop in *Impressions and Landscapes*, where he adopted as his own the seventeenth-century poet Pedro Soto de Rojas's epithet of Granada the 'paradise closed to many'. For the unhappy Federico, Granada was permeated with 'the emptiness of a thing irredeemably finished'. His own sense of loss, the fall from his childhood paradise of innocence and connectedness, found an echo in this modern Granada's divorce from its roots. Interestingly enough, but perhaps not surprisingly, this description of Granada was not included in the original publication of *Impressions and Landscapes*. Another self-imposed silence, of a sort.

So it was that in 1919 Federico persuaded his parents to allow him to spend the coming academic year studying at the University of Madrid and, just as importantly, to live in the Residencia de Estudiantes (the Student Residence situated in Madrid's Calle Pinar, where the Lorca Foundation is housed today). If he was going to succeed as a professional writer, he had little choice but to live in Madrid, and the Residencia de Estudiantes promised an enabling and liberal atmosphere. Set up in 1915 (although there had been an earlier trial period dating from 1910), the Residencia was to have an unprecedented influence on Spanish art and literature right up until its enforced closure in 1936. According to one of the students who had resided there, José Bello, the enormous success of the Residencia was due to the fact that this was the only coherent and sustained educational project ever to be developed in Spain which maintained itself free from Church influence.[2] In that sense, the Residencia was the logical culmination of a whole strand of Spanish nineteenth-century liberalism, well organized, efficient and liberating. Its staggering list of visiting lecturers reads like an early twentieth-century who's who, among them Wells, Keynes, Chesterton, Claudel, Le Corbusier, Valéry, Aragon... the world's avante-garde, as well as established artists and thinkers, who came to the Residencia to add their own ingredients to the place's own heady mix of intellectual curiosity and cultural experimentation.

Put in these terms, it is clearly less of a coincidence than it seems that Federico should have found himself there at the same time as future artists of the stature of Luis Buñuel and Salvador Dalí. Indeed, given the oasis of liberal education that the Residencia represented, there is something almost of an historical inevitability about it for a variety of reasons. Firstly, liberal-minded families who sought a secular university-level education for their children had little choice other than to consider dispatching their offspring to the Residencia (private hostals and the like were considered dangerous flesh-pots). Secondly, the stimulation that the Residencia provided, in terms of both the intellectual space and the well-endowed facilities that it provided for the residents, as well as its vivid cultural programme, had an inevitable impact on the developing sensibilities of any young man whose interests lay in the arts. Thirdly, Buñuel, Dalí and Lorca all came from well-to-do backgrounds; Buñuel was the son of Aragonese landowners, Dalí from a well-known Catalan legal family, and Lorca, as we have seen, the eldest child of an Andalusian rural businessman. Aragon, Catalonia and Andalusia, a Spain in miniature, and each of these three young men were characteristic products of their very different regions and cultures; the Aragonese solid and earthy, the Catalan innovative and self-regarding, and the Andalusian exuberant but constantly searching for a positive self-image in the eyes of others. All three of them sharing a common and deeply held hostility to the spirit of denial and negation inherent in the Spanish status quo of pious Catholicism and bourgeois moral certainty. And all of them, as they acknowledge in their own writings, already acutely, perhaps even morbidly, aware of the physical reality of death, of a 'death ever present, as it had been since the Middle Ages', as Buñuel wrote.[3] Dalí, the youngest of the three, is the one most tormented by the pervasive evidence of death. Initially, like Federico, his whole sense of identity, as he describes it, is bound up with a death. In this case, rather than Lorca's occasional fantasy of himself as the son of another mother now dead, it is with a deceased sibling that the young Dalí is engaged in posthumous rivalry:

All my eccentricities, all my incoherent exhibitions come from my life's great tragic obsession. I have always wanted to prove that it was me who existed and not my dead brother. Like in the myth of Castor and Pollux, by killing my brother, I could win my own immortality.[4]

The link in Dalí's mind between death and sexuality is also the most explicit and, without any doubt, the most disabling. His inability to view sexuality without the most profound cancer of guilt, invariably followed by the stench of decay and death, is expressed more graphically than anything we find in Lorca or Buñuel. Apparently, Dalí's father was obsessed with the idea that he, like the respectable bourgeois father in Ibsen's *Ghosts*, may have been responsible for the death of Dalí's elder brother as a result of the sexual excesses of his earlier days. Dalí recalled in an interview published in 1979 that his father took draconian action so that he, his next son, should not fall into the same abyss:

> My father left a book of medicine on top of the piano, full of photographs of the most appalling consequences of venereal diseases. I was terrified [...] When I went to Paris for the first time [...] I visited a whole succession of brothels. And with each one of the whores there I observed the same ritual. I asked them to stand at the farthest end of the room, so that any germs there might have been about her person would not be able to get anywhere near me. All I did was look at her while I masturbated. So it's quite clear that it is possible to nourish and to enjoy extraordinary sexual passion and pleasure without having to risk the slightest carnal contact.[5]

To judge from this, and other anecdotes which Dalí recounts about his subsequent relationships, his father's tactic was strikingly effective. Buñuel, who also partook of the services of brothels, although with a more active relish, must have known of this story long before it was finally published in the *Playboy* interview of 1979. One of his finest films, *Belle de jour*, features a similar scene in which an absurdly scrupulous stranger forces the character played by Catherine Deneuve to take off her clothes at a similar arm's length. Inevitably then, the three young men discussed and made art from their obsessive association of sex with death. In a country where death is traditionally represented in all its gruesome reality – visitors to the museums of Spanish cathedrals, for example, can testify to that – Buñuel, Dalí and Lorca display the most extraordinary images of the decay of the flesh in their work. Interestingly, they also relate this physical decay to the moral and spiritual putrefaction of the Spanish middle classes, constantly alluding to them as *los putrefactos* ('the putrefied'), and thereafter frequently pillorying them in their work.[6]

LORCA AND BUÑUEL IN THE RESIDENCIA, 1922

Intimate Strangers

Buñuel was the first to arrive at the Residencia, living there from 1917 to 1925, the year in which he moved to Paris. Although Lorca was two years his senior (and five years older than Dalí), the young Andalusian did not take up residencia until 1919, remaining there also until 1925 (although he returned frequently right up until 1928). Dalí arrived in 1922, and lived in the Residence until he was finally and ignominiously expelled from the San Fernando College for the Fine Arts in 1926. Buñuel recalls Lorca's arrival at the Residencia in his autobiographical *My Last Breath* (my translation):

> *Federico García Lorca didn't arrive at the Residencia until two years after me...* *Brilliant, hugely likeable, distinctly elegant with his impeccable tie, a look that was dark and shining at the same time, Federico was attractive to everyone. He had a personal magnetism that no one could resist.*[7]

On the surface, however, it would have seemed that Lorca and Buñuel did not actually have that much in common. Buñuel was an ardent sportsman, a devotee of boxing, while Lorca was actively uninterested in any sort of recreational exercise, no doubt the result of a slight limp that he had had since childhood – it was said that no one ever saw him break into anything beyond a moderately paced walk. Moreover, Buñuel's brand of heterosexuality was an openly aggressive one:

> *When we were young, we couldn't stand pederasts [the literal translation of Buñuel's original]. [...] I even acted as an agent provocateur in a Madrid toilet. My friends used to wait outside, and I would go in and play the bait. One evening, a man bent over towards me. We gave the poor wretch a good hiding when he went out. It just seems absurd today.*[8]

Federico would undoubtedly have been aware of this unpalatable aspect of his friend's nature (although it is impossible to imagine him giving approval to

this sort of incident). Another anecdote is particularly telling, permitting us a deep insight into the limitations of the Buñuel–Lorca friendship:

> *Somebody came running to tell me that Martín Domínguez, a Basque lad, was going round saying that Lorca was a homosexual. I couldn't believe it. At that time in Madrid, there were only two or three known pederasts, and there was no reason to suppose that Federico was one of them.*
>
> *We were sitting in the refectory, side by side and facing the presidential table where Unamuno and Eugenio d'Ors [...] happened to be eating that particular day. After the soup, I whispered to Federico:*
>   *'Let's go outside... I have to talk to you about something very serious'.*
> *He was surprised, but agreed. We stood up.*
> *We were given permission to go out before finishing lunch. We went to a nearby bar. As soon as we went in, I told Federico I was going to have to fight Martín Domínguez, the Basque.*
>   *'Why?', Lorca asked.*
> *I hesitated for a second. I didn't know what to say. Then I blurted out:*
>   *'Is it true you're a pansy?'*
> *He stood up, wounded to the quick, and said:*
>   *'You and I are finished'.*
> *And off he went.*
> *Of course, we made up that very same evening. There was nothing effeminate about Federico, not the slightest affectation.*[9]

Later on, of course, Buñuel was to admit that Federico was indeed homosexual. But he always found it difficult to accept the fact, and the anecdote is left deliberately ambiguous. Indeed, one of the seeds of discord which were later sown into his relationship with Dalí was precisely the fact that the painter had taken to openly referring to Lorca as 'the pederast' [once again, a literal translation] thereby letting, in Buñuel's eyes, the shameful cat out of the bag. Of course, the Residencia was a characteristically self-regarding student society where image was of crucial importance, and Buñuel would have been far from immune to the pressures to conform to the stereotypical image of heterosexuality. But if we are to take the story at face value, and to judge by some of Lorca's more intimate confessions around that time, Federico also felt constrained by the same pressures. Not that he was able to fool all of the residents all of the time. A contemporary recalled 'not everyone liked him. One or two of them sniffed out his defect and they kept their distance from him'.[10] Given the prejudices of his time, Federico could not have expected to find a genuinely liberal environment anywhere, even in the famed Residencia de Estudiantes. Nevertheless, he would have had a very clear idea of those to whom he could talk intimately and those that he couldn't. Luis Buñuel would have belonged to the second group.

Which is not to say that they did not enjoy a fruitful and mutually beneficial relationship. Each found the other exhilarating, exulting in the rebellious and subversive spirit which would come to characterize their work, and exploring their far-reaching interest in a variety of different forms and media. Together they explored the ancient world of puppetry, the exciting new world of the cinema, the various expressions of the avante-garde that came surging into the Residencia... they were young intellectual radicals living to the full one of the most exciting moments in Spanish cultural history.[11] Buñuel has never disguised the fact that had it not been for his relationship with Federico, he certainly would not have abandoned his studies in Agrarian Engineering in favour of an Arts degree, and that he would almost certainly not have begun to develop his own literary interests. However, both Lorca and Buñuel would also have been aware of a silence at the heart of their friendship. They had already been friends for nearly three years when the extravagant figure of Salvador Dalí arrived to take up residence. And that silence became more problematic.

Buñuel writes that it was he who first recognized Dalí's ability as a painter, having stumbled across him working in his room. And it was he who introduced him to the group of friends. Whatever the reasons underlying

Buñuel's proprietorial claims, it rapidly became clear that the mercurial Catalan and the exuberant Andalusian were deeply drawn to each other. In the first stages of this developing relationship, Buñuel seemed inseparable from them, in great part due to his own professed regard for the sacred codes of friendship. Together they became notorious for their *juergas*, their frequently drunken nights out on the town. But jealousy – sexual, social and artistic – very soon began to infiltrate to the core of the triangle. Lorca's summer visits to Dalí's home in Cadaqués, the aura of sexual ambivalence which hung around their relationship like smoke round a fire, the competition for social and artistic seniority in the Residencia, can all be seen as factors in the deterioration which was eventually in 1927 to lead Buñuel to refer to 'the wretched Federico with his acolyte Dalí in tow'.[12] Thereafter he would devote himself to enticing the Catalan into his own ambit of influence.

In spite of the volume of words that the relationships between Dalí, Lorca and Buñuel have spawned – or perhaps because of them – there are still considerable uncertainties as to the reality of things. A great deal of this doubt arises from the self-regarding nature of their own recollections. In *My Last Breath*, published in 1982, Buñuel ducks and weaves through his relationship with Lorca with the same skills he apparently employed to good effect as a boxer. The result is that very little goes beyond the merely anecdotal, and where issues of Lorca's sexuality do arise, they tend to be obscured by Buñuel's inability or unwillingness to recognize it openly. Dalí's testimony is much more explicit, but riddled with internal contradictions. Some of these may be due to lapses in memory, others perhaps to his well-known love of the sensational, yet others to his conviction that any sort of consistency is the mark of a small mind. There can be little doubt, however, that Lorca was obsessed by Dalí's androgynous beauty. A number of books and articles have coyly chosen to represent their relationship either in terms of an 'intimate conflict' or as a 'loving friendship'.[13] However, in a late interview with Ian Gibson, Dalí admitted that 'it was no simple friendship but a very strong erotic passion'.[14] More movingly, a nurse, who attended him through his grotesque decline in the final stages of his life, subsequently declared in a newspaper interview:

> *The only time I noticed a light in his eyes was once when he moved his lips to say 'my friend Lorca', meaning the poet. In the whole time I was looking after him, that was the only coherent phrase I heard him utter.*[15]

These two declarations have more of a ring of truth about them than the whole series of objectionable comments which the narcissistic Dalí made throughout his life. Three of the most notorious are included in Agustín Sánchez Vidal's *Buñuel, Lorca, Dalí: El enigma sin fin:*

> *Olé! With that traditionally Spanish cry I received in Paris the news that the best friend of my turbulent adolescence had been shot.*

> *I reacted with joy. Anyway, my highly developed Jesuitical sensibilities always make me think that when one of my friends dies, that it was me who killed him, that it was my cause he died for.*

> *Naturally enough, I enjoy a sardine much more if I think about my dead friends when I'm eating it, especially those who have been shot or martyred.*[16]

Whether these words represent the attempt to misrepresent his own troubled conscience for not having done more to convince his friend to leave the country as the Civil War loomed, or whether they genuinely constitute an attempt to create distance from a subversive writer at a time when he himself was courting Francoism, what is certainly true is that lurking behind all of these declarations is the obsession with Lorca that accompanied Dalí throughout his life. The truth of these anecdotes probably lies, simply, in his desire to scandalize, to assert himself through the shocked reaction of others. Moreover, his notorious disregard for any type of moral coherence and his flaunting of the bonds of friendship had already led to a violent encounter

BUÑUEL AND LORCA IN A FAIRGROUND PHOTOGRAPH, MADRID, 1920's

with Buñuel in New York just after the Civil War. It seems likely, however, that close to death something of the truth of that all-consuming and brilliant relationship had resurfaced in his memories.

Whether or not that relationship was ever consummated is, of course, much more difficult to assess. It seems eminently likely that it was. Dalí himself referred to two failed attempts at sexual intercourse when he generously decided that Lorca's prestige and brilliance were such that 'he was owed a bit of the ass of the Divine Dalí'.[17] But all of this courts the danger of descending into the archaeology of gossip. The facts of their sexuality are of less interest than are their reasons for concealing it. And what is of immediate interest here is the great work that came about as a direct result both of their passion and of the envy that such passion provoked.

Perhaps the first major work of tribute to be produced by a member of this uneasy trinity was Lorca's 'Ode to Salvador Dalí', finally published in 1926. The poem, which Lorca had originally wished to call 'Didactic Ode to Salvador Dalí', is in many ways a statement of artistic principle, a celebration of an art which is simultaneously passionate and precise. The opening lines will give a flavour:

A rose in the high garden of your desire.
A wheel on the pure syntax of steel.
The mountain emerging naked from impressionist mist.
The greys hoisting their final balustrades.

And modern painters in their white rooms
Cut the aseptic flower of the square root.
A marble iceberg in the waters of the seine
Freezing window panes, cutting the ivy away.

These are images drawn from Dalí's own paintings, reflecting his and Lorca's shared desire for clarity of line and measure. But in terms of voice, its accumulation of separately striking images, the poem also re-creates the powers of Dalí's visual imagination, his ability to reach deep below the surface of the conscious mind in order to pull out and conceptualize visually the dark forces brooding there. This is an art which is clear-sighted, sweeping away the obfuscations of the Impressionists. Its lucidity cuts with surgical precision through to the depths of the psyche. No gentle lingering on the surface of the real here. In this way, the poem also heralds the commitment to the avant-garde and to experimentation with form and expression which were to remain with Lorca throughout his life. The qualities he attributes to the artist Dalí here were qualities he would also make his own.

Buñuel, Lorca and Dalí, like many other young artists of their moment, were caught up in the swirl of the avant-garde, all of them in implicit competition to lead the vanguard with increasingly innovative forms and vision. The risk here, as the Spanish philosopher Ortega y Gasset was soon to underline, was that art would become dehumanized, form for form's sake. Lorca's 'Ode' is already aware of such a possibility. Above all else, therefore, this is a poem of love, as its eventual title suggests, 'perhaps the finest paean to friendship ever written in Spanish', as Gibson has written:[18]

> Oh Salvador Dalí, with your olive voice!
> I tell what your person and your paintings tell me,
> Not praising your adolescent brush
> But singing the firm guidance of your arrows...

> But above all else I sing of a common thought
> That unites us in the dark times and in the golden.
> Art is not the light that blinds us,
> But rather love, friendship or the sword.

The final reference to the 'sword' (*esgrima* , 'fencing', in the original) is puzzling. The use of an 'or' which is simultaneously disjunctive and copulative in order to create new readings of reality is a common surrealist device. Taken as a disjunctive, the 'or' perhaps stresses friendship as an alternative to aggressive posturing. But when copulative, it can certainly be read as a reference to the extension of friendship into the realm of the phallic.

The title of Dalí's canvas *Honey is Sweeter than Blood* expresses the same sort of disjunction: friendship or the sword. In many ways, this painting represents Dalí's greatest tribute to Federico. The unmistakable form of Lorca's head is evident in a bust lying on the ground, while critics have identified the more stylized head and the mutilated torso which also appears in the canvas as belonging to Dalí himself and Buñuel respectively. Between them, there is another mutilated torso, this time, significantly, of a female form. Lorca was so taken by the painting that he asked the artist to append his name to it as a guarantee of immortality should his own ambitions come to nothing. Lorca's head and shadow were to appear in a number of subsequent paintings, but *Honey is Sweeter than Blood*, painted in 1927 when their relationship was at its most intense, remains the most powerful of Dalí's tributes. What Federico would certainly have recognized in the painting would have been a version of the tensions between the three friends, and the way in which all of them rejected women: Lorca through his homosexuality, Dalí through his sexual neuroses, Buñuel through the misogyny which was to characterize his cinema.

As Dalí and Lorca grew closer, Buñuel tried to entice Dalí to leave Madrid and join him in Paris. His reasons for doing so inevitably derived from a sort of sibling rivalry, although Buñuel himself would have explained that he was trying to snatch the avante-garde Dalí from the clutches of the decadent Lorca. There can be no doubt that Buñuel's fervent embracing of the surrealist ethic at this time would have distanced him considerably from Lorca, a writer the greater part of whose work at this time derived from a clearly recognizable tradition. And he had no qualms about letting Lorca know how much he disapproved of his work. From an interview with the Spanish writer Max Aub:

> *They were friends, all right. He [Dalí] was much more friendly with Federico than I was. I was friendlier with Dalí than with Federico. I don't like Federico's work at all. His theatre is awful. One or two poems perhaps are okay [...] We arranged once for him to read his* Don Perlimplín *to us... By the end of the first act [..] I said simply 'This is awful'. Federico was furious: 'Well, that's not what Dalí thinks. You don't deserve to be my friend.' And he turned to Dalí and asked 'Isn't that right?' And Dalí replied 'Well, no, it isn't very good.' So Federico jumped up, scooped up his papers and stormed out.*[19]

The tone of triumphalism in the telling of the anecdote is clear. Two victories in one – the artistic and the personal, the dismissive criticism of the play and the weaning away of an intimate but fickle friend.

The same two objectives were realized again in Buñuel's first film, *Un chien andalou*. Made in 1929, the short piece represented an extravagant excursion into surrealism, greatly inspired and gleefully abetted by Dalí. The opening scene of the film remains one of the most memorable in cinema history. There is a rapid sequence of images – a razor being whetted, clouds cutting across the moon, a woman's face in close-up, and finally an eye (in reality, the shaved, made-up eye of a calf) sliced open by the razor. As an exercise in image-making the film is remarkable, announcing the quirky imagism and unconventional genius that were to be the hallmarks of Buñuel's cinema. Lorca, however, immediately took the 'Andalusian dog' of the title as a scornful reference to him. He had many good reasons for doing so. There are taunting references – transvestism and impotence – that he took as being to his own sexuality. This in conjunction with the title might have been enough for Lorca to have felt aggrieved, but the film also abounded in a whole series of images drawn from the three friends' secret language of shared obsessions. Privately then, as well as publicly, the film seemed to be, at the very least, cocking a snoot at the vulnerable Federico. After that relations were inevitably to be strained. They were all only to meet once or twice more after this, and for a space of four years (between 1931 and 1935) Lorca and Dalí didn't meet at all. Less than a year after their final meeting, which took place in October 1935, Lorca would be dead.

Many Different Lorcas

One of the probable intentions of Dalí and Buñuel in excluding him from, and alluding to him in, *Un chien andalou* was to signal their conviction that in the debate between traditionalism and the avante-garde, Federico was resolutely in the wrong camp, that he was a mere folk artist. But just as Lorca was mercurial in his personal life, presenting a whole series of different selves to different people, so even his early work exhibits much more variety of range and form than this dismissive and axe-grinding view allows. As Aleixandre's description of Lorca implies, there was always something ultimately unknowable about the man, or at least an essential dimension of his being to which very few had access. Why Lorca should have shorn up his private life on ramparts of secrecy is quite clear. Aleixandre himself would have had a very different view of Federico than did Buñuel. Federico would often absent himself from his friends at the Residencia to enjoy the more congenial and understanding company of other gay poets like Luis Cernuda who gathered at Aleixandre's house.[20] And all of them were more supportive of Federico's work than either the fervently avante-garde Buñuel or the insecure Dalí.

The Residencia period was certainly a fertile one in terms of Lorca's own writings. Between 1921 and 1924 he wrote the suites of poems published as *First Songs* and *Songs*. In many ways, these echo the tone of *Poem of Deep Song*: they are infused with a sense of loss, a yearning for things out of reach, impossible loves – the stuff of popular song which was also the stuff of Federico's life. For the most part, they move tautly between sharply focused images, once again drawn from the popular musical tradition and the physical reality of Andalusia. But this is writing which, while it sinks its roots into its own home soil, travels far beyond the concerns of a literature centred merely upon the local, no matter what Buñuel and latterly Dalí seemed to think. The poem entitled 'Verlaine' encapsulates the elegiac tone of the collection as a whole, at the same time as pointing to its cause:

> The song
> I shall never tell
> Sleeps upon my lips.
> The song
> I shall never tell.
> Over the honeysuckle
> A firefly,
> A moonshaft spears
> The water.

And then I dreamt
The song
I shall never tell.

A song full of lips,
Of distant flows.

A song full of hours
Lost in shadow.

A song of a living star
In a perpetual day.

There are readings of this poem which have suggested that it is the poet's vain reaching for the essentially ineffable aspects of human experience, which is expressed in the 'song/I shall never tell'. In that respect, the poem is taken as a meditation on the way in which it is music rather than language which is most capable of expressing our intimate world (hence the reference to Verlaine: *la musique avant toute chose*). An alternative reading, however, might be that Lorca is lamenting the silence which he must impose upon his sexuality (hence the reference to Verlaine, lover of Rimbaud). This reading is reinforced by the spectacular image of cosmic penetration as the moonlight pierces the water. 'Moon' and 'water', both feminine nouns in Spanish, are images of a non-genderized sexuality which are frequent in Lorca's work, simultaneously subjects and objects of the deep-rooted pan-eroticism that began to flower in *Impressions and Landscapes*. One of their most potent conjunctions occurs in the final scene of *Yerma*. Set during a carnivalesque pilgrimage, when barren and unmarried women have come to drink 'from the river of men', it features Yerma's outraged slaying of her husband, Juan. Having confirmed to her that she will never have children with him, but that he still desires her because 'you look lovely under the moon', Yerma is transformed into an avenging principle. Like the goddess Diana who comes to earth to avenge the intrusive lust of man (in the form of Acteon), Yerma's link with the moon reminds us of the huge and dangerous force of nature baulked.[21] Her killing of her husband represents nature at its purest destroying a sullied heterosexuality whose means and ends have little to do with love. In the 'Ode to Walt Whitman', in *Poet in New York*, Lorca would attack the representatives of a tainted homosexual love for exactly the same reasons.

One of the simplest and most moving poems of *Songs* echoes Yerma's grief, the sense of loss that comes from sterility. In 'Song of the Dry Orange Tree', the central image is characteristically Lorquian, one of nature denied:

> Woodcutter.
> Cut my shadow away.
> Free me from the pain
> Of seeing myself without fruit.
>
> Why was I born among mirrors?
> The day spins me round
> And the night copies me
> In all its stars.
>
> I want to live blind to myself.
> And the ants and buzzards
> I shall dream
> Are my leaves and birds.
>
> Woodcutter.
> Cut my shadow away.
> Free me from the pain
> Of seeing myself without fruit.[22]

Lyrical, tormented. A poet protesting at the injury done when nature is denied. Undoubtedly as well, a gay man who adored children lamenting his own condemnation to childlessness. The imaginative link with both Yerma and the mother who might have been, Matilde Palacios, is patent. In the image of the tree haunted by its own shadow, we also sense Lorca's distaste at having to play himself in front of himself, of being the spectator of the self-projections which are distortions of his hidden core.

Some of Lorca's most popular poems – in both senses of that adjective – are to be found in this lyrically elegiac collection. Death is indeed omnipresent, like a character stalking the emotional landscape of the poems. But they are poems which sing the pain, which suggest that whatever personal traumas are being played out here, the redemptive and restorative power of art is already at work. In the apparently simple poem 'Farewell', an intimation of death, the skull beneath the skin, is offset by images which celebrate the here and now of the life of the senses:

> If I die,
> Leave the balcony open.
>
> The child is eating oranges.
> From my balcony I can see him.
>
> The reaper reaps the corn.
> From my balcony I can hear him.
>
> If I die,
> Leave the balcony open!

This is moving and effective, the emblematic lyric of a poet always on the side of life. But suicide, a desire for the peace of nothingness, is also a recurrent motif in Lorca's work – whether the result of the raging despair of Adela in *The House of Bernarda Alba*, or, as in this poem from *Songs*, a desire to escape from the guilt of selfhood:

Suicide
(perhaps because you didn't learn your geometry)

The young boy had forgotten himself.
It was ten in the morning.

His heart was filling
With broken wings and flowers of rags.

He felt on his lips
The one word that remained.

And taking off his gloves,
A rain of soft ash fell.

From his balcony a tower could be seen,
And he was both balcony and tower.

And without doubt he saw
The clock watching him, unmoving in its case.

And he saw his shadow lying still
On a divan of white silk.

And the young boy, rigid, geometric,
Shattered the mirror with an axe.
And as he did, a great spurt of shadow
Filled the unreal room.

This is a poem which vividly encapsulates the preoccupations of Federico, now in his early twenties, although the boy referred to in the poem is clearly some years younger. One thing should be clear from the outset, however. This is not a poem that reasserts the literary cliché of the romanticized association of homosexuality with suicide. The suicide here is a metaphorical one; the shadow which invades the room is an intimation of death, or death of a sort. The image of the mirror and axe is a clear echo of 'Song of the Dry Orange Tree', an indication perhaps that whatever crisis the young boy is suffering, it is caused at least in part by a growing awareness of sterility (hence the references to broken wings, flowers made from rags, ash etc.). The reference to the tower and the ungloved hands with their rain of ash (the Spanish slang word for ejaculated semen is 'dust') perhaps suggests masturbation, with its accompanying baggage of guilt (the 'spurt of shadow') and its overtones of lonely solitude ('an unreal room'). The stopped clock reinforces the intensity of the moment that the boy is living, but this is an intensity which is both sterile and deeply complex. For he is both upright tower and open balcony, male and female elements in a tension whose only fruit is guilt and incomprehension. The young boy smashes his image in the mirror as an act of self-loathing, a self-punishment inflicted on himself, 'grotesque and without solution'. What he is killing is one of the two selves he has been forced to inhabit, driven by the knowledge gained from the mirror that he is both one and other. He has failed to reconcile the warring elements of his being, the sexual tensions, the internal and external versions of his personality, the wish to procreate and the awareness that he never will. Torn between desire and guilt, he has failed to learn the rules of balance and measure, the geometry that keeps us all intact.

If we assume, as seems most probable, that this poem was written while Lorca was at the Residencia, it gives a clear indication that, even then, he remained locked into an emotionally charged analysis of his sexually formative years (another meaning, perhaps, for the stopped clock in 'Suicide'). But it would be a mistake to assume that this suite of generally introspective poems was the only voice or sole form of his work at that time. He was also beginning to turn his attention to the theatre. There were a number of obvious reasons why he should have done so – not least among them being his own constant exuberant performance of self. His early love of the ritual of the mass, the colour, the costume and the incense, had been sharpened by visiting theatre companies, travelling puppet shows and so on. He had begun to write dialogues and short plays in his late teens, and around 1922, prompted by the musician Manuel de Falla, had adapted an old Andalusian folk tale, *The Girl Who Watered the Basil*, as a puppet play.[23] And even as a poet he was passionately committed to the notion of the word in performance, and there are a number of enthusiastic testimonies of the delight he took in reading his plays and poems to groups of friends. For Federico, poetry was always in the air, not pinned like a butterfly to the page.

He tended to claim that his first play to be performed was *Mariana Pineda*, premiered in Madrid's Teatro Goya in 1927.[24] The eponymous heroine was a well-known historical figure who had been executed in the early nineteenth century for embroidering the flag of liberal Spain. Lorca, however, reinvents her not as the sacrificial victim of a political cause, no matter how appealing that cause would undoubtedly have proved to him, but as a woman of flesh and blood who knowingly dies for the man she loves. The play is word-heavy, a typical first play (almost) from the pen of a poet, and critics have tended to treat it as a thing apart in his body of work. In one sense, it is. Lorca wrote no other historical dramas, nor did he ever again treat a theme which was so explicitly linked to the politics of Spain (even though the work stands as a statement of the inauthenticity of political life). But it is not difficult to see how Lorca's later theatre develops from this early piece. Not solely in the simple sense of his work as a celebration of impossible and defeated love, but in a more general way, in terms of the overall project to which his work is committed: the reconstruction of a spiritual as well as historical homeland, the defence of a way of being that was radically different from the hostile otherness which was the dominant experience he had had of public life to date.

Of course, *Mariana Pineda* was not, in fact, his first play to be professionally

staged. He, perhaps conveniently, tended to overlook the premiere (again in Madrid) in 1920 of his *The Butterfly's Evil Spell*, a short play which attracted mainly derision from the Madrid critics and was withdrawn after just a few performances.[25] Years later Lorca was to tell his friend the poet Rafael Alberti that he had treated the whole thing as a laughing matter, but this kind of bravado would not be untypical of Lorca's self-protective instinct. It is easy to suggest that the short play was panned because of its radically innovative – for Spain, at least – storyline: a host of insects playing out a tale of unrequited love. But the play is over-written and at times cloying. There is some gentle humour, but the intensity of the characteristically Lorquian theme – 'the sad tale of one who reached for the moon and found only what it is to have a broken heart' – is hopelessly distanced and diluted by the fact that it is played out by characters who are beetles, fireflies, butterflies and the like. Interestingly though, the play begins with a prologue spoken directly to the audience which indirectly highlights the relationship between the play's central situation and its author's sense of disassociation from his own community and its mating rituals. Once again at the heart of everything is the sense of the fall from grace, the loss of connectedness:

> *Love, the same love that passes through human lives with its ironies and tragedies, this time visits a far-off meadow inhabited by insects – where, once upon a time, life was peaceful and serene [...] But one day there was an insect who yearned to go beyond this sort of love, who was filled with a vision very different to the normal run of life.*

Two much more significant plays were also being written during Lorca's time at the Residencia. One of them in particular stands out, the extraordinarily understated *The Love of Don Perlimplín for Belisa in the Garden*, which he began in 1926. As we have seen, it received the undeserved, but nonetheless wounding, derision of Buñuel and Dalí (and, incidentally, the wrath of the censor). Described graphically by its author as an 'Erotic Strip Cartoon', the short play has a very strong *commedia dell'arte* feel about it, with its unequal marriage between the beautiful young Belisa and the withering fifty-year old Perlimplín, aided and abetted by a worldly wise servant and grasping mother.[26] The story, with its final moment of bitter and unexpected recognition, when Belisa discovers that her cuckolded husband is also her secret lover, once again reveals Lorca's taste for dramatizing the powerful emotions which tear through human life. But Don Perlimplín, 'parcel of puss and lust', as he calls himself in the moment of self-disgust which comes in the wake of his realization that he has allowed the best of his life to drift meaninglessly by out of fear of real engagement, is elevated to a Christ-like status. His passion and inevitable sacrifice in the garden clearly indicate this. But it is his determination to live beyond the accepted morality of the herd when he proudly sings 'Don Perlimplín has no honour' that gives him his genuinely transcendental value in Lorca's eyes. This is Perlimplín's great refusal, the moment when the sacrificial Christ becomes the messianic sower of discord in his community. It is his version of the poet's 'How can my heart be held to blame?' Interestingly enough, one of Lorca's earliest (but incomplete) dramas, written around the same time as *Book of Poems*, was entitled *Christ*, and develops his own identification with precisely this view of the subversive and revolutionary impact of love in a rigidly codified society.

The other play upon which Federico was working around this time was *The Shoemaker's Wonderful Wife*. Like *Don Perlimplín,* this play was not finally completed until four or five years later. Lorca typically worked this way, either returning obsessively to manuscripts upon which he had been working – as in the case of these two plays – or mulling over for years the nub of a story before feverishly spilling it on to the page – as with *Blood Wedding*. *The Shoemaker's Wonderful Wife* once again features an example of the strong-willed woman who is capable of dominating all around her (Don Perlimplín actually makes a garbled reference to her in justification of his fearful withdrawal from life). On one level, this may be an echo of the figure of the stern, authoritarian mother. But more central to the shoemaker's wife and to Belisa is an unease

LORCA AND DALÍ IN CADAQUÉS IN THE SUMMER OF 1927

not simply as to woman as siren, the embodiment of a crudely conceived homosexual distaste, but more roundly about the power of love to intrude massively into the routine of the individual life. Where Lorca's sexuality perhaps most directly shapes these two plays, in a manner which looks forward to his more mature pieces, is in his rejection of the form and conditions of marriage. This is precisely why the shoemaker's wife is wonderful. Like Perlimplín, she is able and willing to pursue her own vital interests above and beyond the call of an honour code which never amounts to anything much more than the prying eyes and chattering tongues of neighbours.

For all of their sense of theatrical experimentation and sheer linguistic and dramatic verve, for all of their radical condemnation of love locked away or codified into society's harsh institutions and empty strictures, these are plays which present varying degrees of aesthetic shielding from their central conflict. Indeed, throughout this whole period of Lorca's life, his creativity is concerned with describing and investigating dramatic situations and forms of cultural expression which bear only an oblique relationship to his own situation rather than directly addressing it. Given the direct pressures, social, cultural and personal, which were making themselves felt in his life, it is not surprising that this should be so. In 1998, during the centenary celebrations, Manuel Fernández Montesinos argued that an excessive attention to Lorca's homosexuality would have precluded his access to international acclaim.[27] The view is open to some debate. What is true, however, is that his popular success within the Spain of the time would have been massively curtailed had Federico not found alternative voices, such as that of deep song, for the deeply personal vision that was the fruit of his pain. There again, such transformation of experience and emotion, through an aesthetic sleight of hand, is one of the defining elements of all worthwhile artistic endeavour.

Hiding in the City of the Gypsies

Federico had always felt that the gypsies of Spain, in particular those who had settled in Andalusia, had been both guardians and vibrant transmitters of the culture of deep song. His interest in the gypsies was therefore primarily a cultural one, in that the voice and preoccupations of their defining expression echoed and resonated powerfully in his own life and work. But, in their everyday freedom, achieved and maintained at the price of constant social disapproval and ostracization, he also found a telling version of his own fears and aspirations. So, by the mid-1920s, he was already working on a number of poems revolving around gypsy-related themes. Their publication in reviews and magazines provoked an extraordinary degree of public interest, so that by early 1928, when they finally appeared in completed book form as the *Gypsy Ballads*, their success with critics and public alike was well and truly assured.[28] This was the book which was to establish the by now thirty-year old Lorca as one of the leading poets in the Spanish-speaking world. The richly dramatic tone of the poems in which rapid dialogue is slotted into vividly imagistic narrative sections, in keeping with the ballad tradition, captured a wide audience. Even today, *Gypsy Ballads* provides some of the most genuinely popular, most frequently quoted, poems in the Spanish language. In many ways, it is a book which extended the appeal of poetry in Spain (just as *Blood Wedding* four years later would seek to widen the theatre-going public's taste for tragedy). Lorca poured his anguish and obsessive regard for death into the traditional ballad form, kept alive in popular Spanish culture through a whole series of well-known songs and poems (Spanish equivalents of Noyes's 'The Highwayman'), re-creating in the process the central concerns of deep song in tightly written and eminently performable pieces. And although Dalí felt that the book was an irresponsible poetic anachronism, its penchant for quirky, at times surreal, imagery and its tendency to cut and paste observed reality into a reorganized, virtually Cubist, representation, give it an unmistakably modern feel.

Dalí's criticism was to wound Lorca deeply. Moreover, paradoxical though it may seem, he was not wholly overjoyed at the huge public acclaim that his book received. This was, in part, because fame and recognition brought their own intensification of his sense of the bad faith that lay at the heart of his public performance, and in part because he felt that many readers were responding solely to the colourful surface of the *Gypsy Ballads*. In a way, a section of his public was turning him into the 'gypsy poet'. And he himself was by now aware of the whole process of gypsyfication which was beginning to bear upon perceptions of his character and of his work. Not surprisingly, he was keen to restore his artistic credentials by stressing the complexity of the conceptual problem that lies at the heart of the book, emphasizing that the reality conceived and represented there was poetic rather than sociological. In that way, his description of the *Gypsy Ballads* as 'an altarpiece for all of Andalusia' should not be taken as a celebration of local colour any more than Synge's Aran plays can be considered mere evocations of island life or Yeats's poetry an apology for the Celtic Twilight. Rather, if one imagines a baroque Spanish altarpiece, like the splendid example in Salamanca Cathedral, upon which a whole series of individually vivid vignettes combine to tell the entire story of the Gospels, the phrase refers to a reordering of reality, a particular way of distributing the different planes of both the story and its meaning. In the case of the *Gypsy Ballads*, the story is a conceptual one (as the poet himself implied when he referred somewhat tetchily to the gypsies as 'only pegs'). It is the deeply personal clash between those areas of human experience which have been socialized into learnt codes and those which remain resolutely free, symbolized respectively by the Civil Guard and the Gypsies. Each individual poem, like each panel on the altarpiece, both illustrates and extends the range of this central theme. The emotional terrain across which both the gospel story depicted on the altarpiece and the deliberately timeless confrontation of gypsies and Civil Guard take place is the same in both cases. *Gypsy Ballads* is steeped in a passion which is the inevitable prelude to a death foretold.

Through the figure of the gypsies, in the most direct way, Lorca was depicting his own desire to live a life unencumbered by traditional conventions and strictures, as well as exploring the labyrinths and dark corners of the world of the emotions and instincts more generally. In this panorama, the Civil Guards are an objectified voice for the hostile otherness which his subsequent work was increasingly to probe, and which here he dramatizes in an archetypal Spanish form. His analysis of Spanishness, in the sense of the codes of an officially sponsored national morality that has grown up in the wake of the fall of Al-Andalus, has now begun in serious.[29] But it remains timeless, mythical, not set in any immediately recognizable historical reality, as though the author was choosing to live in a world whose construction was purely an issue of aesthetics. There is a danger inherent in this type of writing, namely that the poems fall into empty pastiche; an excursion from the problems of the self, here and now, into the contrived cultivation of an ancient and popular tradition. In itself this is almost a definition of what it is to be 'folksy', an adjective all too frequently applied to Lorca's work. And it is certainly an apt description of the derivative response to Lorca of no small number of writers, theatre directors and translators who have managed only to re-create his work in the image of that folksiness.

Gypsy Ballads gloriously avoids such pitfalls, partly through the sheer verve of the writing, partly through the fact that the shards of pain from the shattering of the wholeness of his emotional world constantly pierce through the fabric of the poems themselves. As a result they re-create a world which is both mysterious and animate, a world inhabited by a consciousness which is both pre-civilized and pre-rational. Civilization – Spanish and Catholic – and reason, the law and the socialized self, are the great enemies of the heart's desire to be free.

The key poem both in this respect, and of the collection as a whole, is the powerful 'Ballad of the Spanish Civil Guard'. Its opening section, as a detachment of the notorious paramilitary force descends menacingly upon the unsuspecting city of the gypsies, is a superb denunciation of the culture of violence:

Black are the horses.
The horseshoes are black.
On their capes shine
Stains of ink and wax.
Their skulls are of lead,
So they cannot weep.
With their patent-leather souls,
They come down the road.
Hunchbacked and nocturnal,
Wherever they breathe they command
Silences of dark rubber
And fears of fine sand.
They pass, if they wish to pass,
And hide in their heads
A vague astronomy
Of half-dreamt pistols.

They are the incarnation of a life-choking bureaucracy (the ink in which the butterfly drowns in 'Back from a Walk'), of an inhumanity (skulls of lead and patent-leather souls; the latter is an allusion to their distinctive three-cornered hat) which imposes a stifling silence and creates a fear so pervasive that it can be likened to the fine sand that creeps into every nook and cranny of the house. They are dark but still recognizable, embodiments of the ambition to control and to destroy. In their astronomy, their sense or vision of the universe, they aspire not to the stars, but to the weaponry and violent trappings of authority. And therefore these guardians of the civil law are creatures of a horror which is typified by darkness and deformity (their hunchbacked nature being a reference to the silhouette of a Civil Guard wearing a backpack).

The quotation gives a representative idea of the style of the collection as a whole. The images are powerfully drawn from an observable physical reality, which in this case is the relentless column of Civil Guards marching down on

Jérez de la Frontera, the city of the gypsies. But of course Jérez de la Frontera is, in reality, not the city of the gypsies. It is in fact the wealthy centre of the sherry and brandy industries. Moreover, no explanation is given for the brutal attack which follows, and in which a number of gypsies, disguised variously as Saint Joseph, the Virgin Mary, exotic sultans, among others, are viciously put to the sword. The key lines occur towards the end of the poem:

> But the civil guard
> Advances sowing flame
> Where, naked and young,
> The imagination burns.

This is one of the very few instances of an abstract noun occurring in the book, and it stands out accordingly. After all, one of the most notable poetic achievements of Lorca's poetry is the way in which it communicates deep emotional states through details of the physical world. What is under attack here, then, is the imagination. There is still a rooting in physical reality, in that the wealthy bourgeoisie of the town are dressed up in order to take part in the traditional Twelfth-night parade in which the central players in the birth of Christ dance and flounce their way through every town and village in Spain, to the delight of the local children. Presumably, the attack of the Civil Guard is the undermining of this experience through a sudden explosion of rationally inspired self-ridicule, the codified self clipping the wings of the non-codified. This ties in with one of the central themes of the collection: this is a world where one of our only redeeming realities is the domain of imagination, a realm which is constantly under the threat of rational dissolution and mechanistic breakdown. The conclusion of the poem is accordingly a lament for that childlike ability to lose oneself in the world of play, as well as clearly signalling Lorca's belief that one of the central objectives of cultural creation should be to reorientate us to the redemptive powers of the ludic:

Oh, city of the gypsies!
Who could have looked upon you only to forget?
Let them search for you on my brow.
The play of moon and sand.

The final identification between poet and gypsy city, however, is not solely the indication of a source of creativity. It is another telling example of Lorca's identification with the defeated; what has happened to this mythical community has happened, in its own way, to him.

This is a collection in which the imagination is protagonist. Where it is curtailed, as in the case of the gypsy nun, it leads to a radical impoverishment. From her window, an unreal, Dalí-like landscape speaks of her repressed sexuality. Her imagination is held tightly in check as she religiously embroiders a straw-coloured cloth. It is left to the poet to give voice to this repressed but throbbing (or throbbing and therefore repressed) world of desire:

A final and muted sound
Shivers through her shirt,
And as she gazes on mountains and clouds
In the lifeless distance,
Her heart of sugar and verbena slowly breaks.
The plain erect
With twenty suns burning above!
The rivers standing upright,
All glimpsed in her fantasy!
But she continues with her flowers,
Whilst upright in the breeze,
The light plays chess
In the high lattice window.

In a curious way, she is a forerunner of Yerma, yet another in a whole series of frustrated women denied love. Typically, Yerma is first presented to us when she is also sewing, an image of the daily drudgery which speaks of freedoms denied. And just as Yerma's tragically reduced sense of marriage is based on her simple acceptance of the contractual exchange of female sexuality for the rights of family and name, so the nun's rational self-control reduces the colour of her imaginative world to black and white – the simplicity of her convictions expressed through the image of light streaming through a lattice window (thus the reference to the squares of the chess board). The game of chess, itself another version of the geometry which eludes the young boy in 'Suicide', is also a metaphor for the onslaught of rational self-control under which her vision and imagination wither.

It was a game of chess with which Lorca himself was familiar on a daily basis. We have already seen that in other poems he intensifies the feeling of self-repression into one of suicide or murder (the damage done to the self at the behest of majority codes and values). This idea underpins, although not without a high degree of self-irony, the pair of poems about the gorgeous gypsy Antoñito el Camborio. Here Lorca's tendency to describe male beauty through elements of the natural world – flowers, fruit, the moon, animals, etc. - is very much to the fore. Antoñito, 'swarthy with green moon', with 'his voice of manly carnation', is arrested by a patrolling pair of Civil Guards for tossing lemons into a roadside pond, turning it into shimmering gold in the process. As a result, in the second of the poems, he is murdered by his cousins for having besmirched the family honour, although Little Anthony, as his name translates, attributes their crime to the fact that:

> What they didn't envy in others
> They envied in me.
> Shoes the colour of purple corinth,
> Jewelry of pure ivory
> And this fine complexion
> Caressed with olive and with jazmine.

Antoñito, in his own view at least, is murdered because of his difference. His awareness of himself verges on the camp, presenting a deliberate subversion both of the canon of male representation and of heterosexual maleness. The poet himself intervenes at the moment of death:

> Oh Antoñito El Camborio,
> Worthy of an empress!
> Remember the virgin
> For you are about to die.
> Oh Federico Garcia,
> Call the civil guard!
> For my waist has snapped
> Like a stalk of corn.

The fact that Antoñito calls for the Civil Guard is a witty version of Lorca's own sense of bad faith, namely that he is frequently forced into the public embracing of values and attitudes that are not his own. But why was the beautiful young gypsy arrested in the first instance? The nature of his crime, the appropriation of fallen lemons, is surely not a heinous one in an Andalusia where lemons are so common that they tend to be left to rot where they lie. Once again, therefore, what is at stake here is really the force of imagination with which Antoñito renders the humdrum (or the essential bitterness) of everyday life into the marvellous and beautiful. It is this power of imagination, with its untrammelled capacity to transform the direction and quality of our lives, which calls down upon itself the wrath of the forces of conformist living.

A gallery of memorable, dramatically etched characters fills the *Gypsy Ballads* with a fabulous range of competing emotions and instincts: the warring gypsies and Civil Guards of 'Knife Fight', where the trailing blood 'moans the serpent's muted song'; the little boy who becomes just another boy as he is hypnotized into adult sexuality by the flamenco dance of a woman as beautiful and mysterious as the moon, 'moving her arms/and showing, lubricious and pure,/her breasts of hard tin'; the lonely gypsy woman, Soledad Montoya who embodies the anguish of the unloved in 'Ballad of the Black Sorrow'; the three sensuously described patron saints of the great trilogy of Andalusian cities, Granada, Seville and Córdoba; Amnon, son of David, who rapes his sister Thamar, another example of illicit love... Perhaps the best loved and possibly the most mysterious of all of the poems is 'Sonambule Ballad', in which a smuggler arrives at his beloved's house only to be told by her father that she is now dead. It is a poem which evokes life's energy and tragedy simultaneously, not making any sense of either, but presenting them in the most moving way possible as the mystery we all live:

> Green, green, I love you green.
>> Green the wind, green the bough.
>> The ship on the sea
>> And the horse on the mountain brow.
>> With shadow at her waist
>> She dreams on her balcony,
>> Green flesh, green hair,
>> With eyes of cold silver.
>> Green, green, I love you green.
>> Under the gypsy moon,
>> Things are watching her
>> Things she cannot see.

This is a poem about life's energy lost. It ends in cinematic style as the young smuggler discovers his dead lover waiting for him inside the house:

>> Over the cistern's face,
>> The gypsy girl was rocking.
>> Green flesh, green hair,
>> With eyes of cold silver.

An icicle of moon
Holds her on the water.
The night became as intimate
As a tiny square.
Drunken civil guards
Were banging on the door.
Green, green, I love you green.
Green the wind, green the bough.
The ship on the sea
And the horse on the mountain brow.

The chorus has all the force of a mantra, simultaneously a love song and a calling for death. But at the doors guarding Lorca's own intimate life, the banging of the Civil Guards of conformism and control was becoming unbearable. It was time for a change.

LORCA PHOTOGRAPHED BY DALÍ WHILST HOLIDAYING IN CADAQUÉS

Desire and Perversion

The Dark Flower of Crisis

I don't know why I left. I ask myself the same question a hundred times a day. I look at myself in the mirror in the narrow little cabin, and I don't know who I am. It's as though I were a different Federico.[1]

Lorca arrived in New York on the 25 June 1929, having spent six days at sea on board the S.S. Olympic. In the unusual environment in which he had found himself, undertaking a major journey for which he was linguistically and culturally unprepared, as he himself was aware, it is not surprising that he should have interrogated his own motives over and over again. In his heart of hearts, however, he knew why he had left – a deep artistic crisis rooted in his sense that Dalí's dismissal of the *Gypsy Ballads* as mere gypsy whimsy was perhaps well founded, an unhappy love affair with a sculptor, Emilio Aladrén, whom he had met in the Residencia, but who was by all accounts only interested in furthering his own artistic reputation by associating with people of the stature of Lorca and Dalí, and a growing impatience with having to play the old game of codes and dissimulation in the hothouse of Spanish literary society. Funded by his father, who was growing increasingly puzzled and concerned by his son's evident unhappiness, he had resolved to seek a change. The sense of displacement, geographical now as well as emotional, which was opening up around him, is expressed once again through the image of the mirror and the unfamiliar face that comes to meet him in it. Crisis, artistic, religious, emotional and sexual, gives *Poet in New York* its dominant tone. When the book was finally published in 1940, the poet Juan Larrea (then exiled in Mexico after the Spanish Civil War) referred to the existential crisis which underlies the book's poetic genesis. His opinions, although still perhaps equivocally expressed, are unusually frank for their time:

When he wrote this book, Federico García Lorca was the tortured victim of a deep personal crisis. Everything seems to point to the fact that this crisis was the result of his sexual anomaly. He is an outsider who cannot live happily within a society which insists on dismissing his congenital abnormality as an offensive defect, when in fact it was neither perverse nor indecent.[2]

Other critics and writers, even those who shared his New York experiences with him, are much coyer or simply express frank denial. In his introduction to the American edition of *Poet in New York*, Angel del Río quotes the views of John Crow, later to become Professor John Crow, who shared a dormitory with Lorca during the course of his studies in Columbia University:

I came into intimate contact with Lorca day after day while he was working on Poet in New York, *and if he was experiencing any 'mortal anguish', I am a monkey's uncle. At times he must have felt very lonely, but at other times he drank, necked and caroused like many another young masculine animal, and seemed to have rather a hilarious time doing it. When he settled down to write poetry in the early morning hours of New York, after midnight, it was with the strained voice, the high key, the midnight fervours of nostalgia burning deep in the darkness. And the picture was no salutary sight.*

Angel del Río, who was a genuine friend of Lorca's, gently chides Crow for having been taken in by Lorca's 'histrionic gaiety'. But we must also read between the lines of del Río's words if we are to have any sense of the real causes and contours of Lorca's crisis:

Lorca, played, talked, laughed, made jokes about everything and everybody, but the anguish was a real one, as were also the personal gloom and emotional preoccupations which he lived through during these months. The sources of this emotional crisis are obscure, at least for those who knew him superficially. They touch delicate fibres of his personality, problems which cannot be easily appraised or dismissed, but which left a very real impact on the book.[3]

Whatever the informing details of the crisis were, and, as is the case in much of Lorca's life and work, many of them are shrouded both in critical reticence and his own care not to leave much written testimony of his intimate world, the huge effect of New York on his subsequent work is clear. It was no less than a formative experience as a result of which – particularly through the so-called rural trilogy of *Blood Wedding*, *Yerma* and *The House of Bernarda Alba* – Lorca's deep-rooted sense of crisis becomes the stuff of growing commitment.[4] The year in New York both sharpened Lorca's appetite for drama and gave him a very clear sense of the social responsibilities of the theatre.

New York, Imperfect in its Despair

If we look at Lorca's work in terms of his determination to understand all the forces of denial that we saw at work in the world around him, we can perhaps arrive at a clearer notion of what exactly the importance of New York was for his subsequent writings. New York is perhaps inevitably experienced by any European in terms of its striking difference, even today. But in the context of of Lorca's obsessed investigation of an otherness that is simultaneously social, sexual and political, the city becomes an objective correlative for a hostile urban otherness that is very much of the moment, Lorca's personal wasteland. In that sense, the real title of *Poet in New York* is more accurately, as Lorca himself suggested, 'New York in a poet'.[5] Lorca draws the city into himself, with its febrile but ultimately mechanistic rhythm of life, its relentless pursuit of Mammon as Wall Street crashed, its rejection and marginalization of the blacks, and in doing so he advances his understanding of the human heart of darkness. In the words he was to put into the mouth of Bernarda Alba in 1936, 'The more you know your own illness, the better.'

One of the New York poems which marks a key stage in this artistic advancement is 'New York: Office and Denunciation'. On one level the poem clearly heralds a new social commitment, a moving away from literary forms which linger in the realms of wholly private concerns or an exclusive aestheticism:

> What shall I do then, impose order on landscapes?
> Impose order on loves that later are photographs,
> And later still splinters of wood and mouthfuls of blood?
> No, no...I denounce!
> I denounce the conspiracy
> Of these deserted offices
> Whose agonies are hidden in the dark,
> Which efface the programmes of the forest,
> And I offer myself to be devoured by the starving cattle
> Crying in the valley,
> Where the hudson flows, drunk on oil.

More particularly, the poem announces a determination to sharpen the focus of Lorca's poetic investigation of hostile otherness, drawing it from the realm of myth, of timeless Civil Guards and gypsies, denizens more of the tradition of deep song than of any specific time or place, moving away from the self-consciously *commedia dell'arte* shrouding of characters like Don Perlimplín or the shoemaker's wonderful wife, and instead probing through his art a sense of denial which is tangibly of the moment.

The final image of the poet as sacrificial victim is worth further comment. This is a crucial image which occurs elsewhere in the New York sequence, foregrounded, for example, as we have seen, in the poem which Lorca chose to open the collection, 'Back from a Walk'. But the agents of sacrifice in this later poem are quite different. This is nature twisted out of all recognition. There is clearly an ecological conscience stirring here as Lorca views the violence that the city commits upon nature – 'This is not hell, but a street./Not death, but a fruit shop' – but the final sense of this image is not solely one of ecology, but one of psychology. The natural world – the river, cattle, by definition also, human beings – has been invaded by an otherness – urbanization, materialism, conformity, lack of values – which is the source of conflict, of discord, of oppressive violence. This is what life is really like, and the poet is consciously choosing to assume the role of interrogator of those forces which conspire to deny the ultimate value of life itself. The poet recognizes that it will be a painful, perhaps even dangerous task. Just how painful and dangerous, Lorca himself surely could not have known.

In the same poem, there is a section whose first couple of lines come to assume a virtually emblematic status in the context of Lorca's subsequent work:

> I denounce all those
> Who ignore the other half,
> That half beyond salvation
> Who raise up mountains of cement
> Where the beating hearts
> Of tiny things are forgotten,
> And where we shall all fall
> In the final fiesta of the drills.
> I spit in your face.
> The other half hears me
> As they devour, urinate and fly in their purity,
> Like children in hallways
> Probing with little sticks
> The gaps and the cracks
> Where insects' antennae rust.

The roots of Lorca's personal crisis and the malaise of Western civilization have become one. The 'other half,/that half beyond salvation' is simultaneously the empowered who bring hell to earth in their promotion of a mechanistic capitalism, and the emotionally dead who have lost all sense of childlike connectedness to the world and to their own feelings; these are the unredeemable Civil Guards who sacrifice emotional intensity, the savouring of the uniqueness of their individual identities, to herd values. They are caught in the trap of the modern, and it is with that trap that this newly modern poet must engage.

New York was for Lorca a human and spiritual wasteland. 'Abandoned Church' memorably evokes not just the confusion of public values but also the private disorientation which result from a civilization where the law and the trappings of control and authority are the prime agents of social organization. It is not a poem in which Lorca's homosexuality is apparent. The real issues here are generated by a different alienation. Written not long after seeing the film version of Erich Remarque's harrowing account of the horrors of the Great War, *All Quiet on the Western Front*, the poem is inspired by Lorca's shock – cultural and spiritual – upon discovering the Anglo-Saxon custom of draping churches with the regimental standards and bomb-tattered flags. Images of war, of a distraught father's loss of a son (who at one point inexplicably becomes a daughter), of a grotesquely glimpsed mass in celebration, all combine in a surrealist frenzy to depict a world where religion is no longer sufficient to hold back collective madness or to quell private pain:

> If my son had been a bear,
> I would not have feared the alligator's stealth
> Nor witnessed the sea tethered to trees
> To be ravished and bled by a tumble of troops.
> If my son had been a bear!
> I'll swathe myself in coarse canvas so as not to feel the mosses' cold
> For I know they'll send me another shirt-sleeve and tie;
> But I'll smash the rudder on the mass's hard core
> And then the madness of gulls and penguins will descend
>   upon the stone

And those who sleep and sing on street corners shall say:
He had a son!
A son! A son! A son
Who was his and his alone, because he was his son!
His son! His son! His son!

The madness here is the rage of the poet. His emotional trauma has been thrown into sharp relief by the civilization of which this city is both symbol and future. But there is also a new anger which springs directly from the experience of life in a society which so relentlessly devours its young and then discards them as nonchalantly as though they were 'blackened match-heads'. In this world of organized immolation, mourning is not enough: the necktie and the restored sleeve (the original having been torn off in an act of ritual mourning, one assumes) represent the sublimation of anger into the conventional codes of living. But this is a rage which will not be quiet. This poem is typical of the whole New York collection in that its expression is wholly destabilizing of traditional representation to a degree that remains puzzling even today. But its rupturing of form and of any coherence outside the internalized logic of the speaker is in itself a powerful defence of an individualism which stands in stark opposition to uniformity of type. And in refusing to fall into silence or muted introspection, by embracing a madness that wheels and cries like seagulls, Lorca is announcing his sense that there be another collectivity – the mad and the dispossessed, those who sleep rough and cry out to the heavens on street corners – which may, at the very least, begin to recognize the shared suffering which binds it. The future author of *Blood Wedding*, *Yerma* and *The House of Bernarda Alba*, is beginning to realize that there is an unacknowledged community which is united through suffering as well as an empowered collectivity. 'Abandoned Church' mercilessly re-creates the pity and the fear, and perhaps especially the anger, of our modern living. Lorca the modern tragedian is born.

Singing to the Pure

Lorca's work brims with images, metaphors, icons and references which are recognizable as expressive of a homosexual culture and discourse: in his drawings, for example, Saint Sebastian, sailors and a range of pierrot characters, and in his writings, the constant equation of man with fruit or flowers, references to silence, and the image of the wounded heart, among many others. The whole idea of 'purity' is also part of Lorca's expression of homosexual love. It is a concept which is clearly associated in the poet's mind with a prelapsarian state. In the second poem in the New York collection, '1910 (Interlude)', he recalls the sensations of a time when childhood innocence has not yet begun to yield to adult perceptions:

> Those eyes of mine on the pony's neck,
> On the pierced breast of Saint Rosa asleep,
> On the rooftops of love, moaning under fresh hands,
> Or on the garden where the cats swallowed frogs.

The reference in the final line of the quotation refers, apparently, to the future poet's mother explaining away nocturnal cries of feline pleasure as the sound of cats devouring frogs. There are many anecdotes, as well as poems and other writings, which illustrate Lorca's love of and ability to empathize with children. He celebrated all those beings not yet corrupted by civilization just as he lamented the passing of his own age of innocence. This uncorrupted part of human nature is one of the defining qualities of the central value of purity. In the way purity is lauded by Lorca, it should not be taken as a synonym for a pre-sexuality, but rather as the innocent enjoyment of sexuality, as in a Greek bacchanal (see, for example, the 'Ode to Walt Whitman'). Neither is it a celebration of a discreetly homosexual love, but rather of the 'rooftops of love, moaning under fresh hands', of a pansexuality, the same principle, ludic and erotic, which united men, women, quail and river in the scene from *Impressions and Landscapes*.[6]

It is this sense of purity, snatched back from the narrow definitions proffered by the Church and the *putrefactos*, which brings us into the complex heart of one of the key poems of the collection, the sweeping 'Ode to Walt Whitman'. The great poet of America is celebrated as pure 'not because he is chaste, but because the schism between body and soul, between homosexual practice and spiritual love, has been salvaged, at least in his poetry', in the words of Angel Sahuquillo.[7] But as Paul Binding has also noted, Lorca reproaches the old master with the sad outcome of his American dream, the debasement of nature in the 'New York of mud/New York of wire and death' where 'life is not good, or noble or holy'.[8] Whitman's dream of the union of body and soul, where life and nature are the perfect measure of man, is just that, a dream:

> And you, beautiful Walt Whitman, sleep on the Hudson's shore,
> Your beard to the pole, your hands wide open.
> Your tongue of soft clay or snow, summoning
> Comrades to watch over you, gazelle without flesh.
> Sleep, for nothing remains.

But of course something does remain. Federico is as ever captured by the ineluctable impossibility of things, that inevitable end of everything in death. But meanwhile there is another community alluded to here once again: the 'comrades' who keep Whitman's delicate spirit alive:

> Man may, if he wishes, lead his desire
> Through coral veins or celestial nudes.
> For tomorrow all our loves will be stone, and time
> A breeze which comes sleeping through the trees.

Love *sub specie aeternatatis*. The cleansing of the doors of perception, to paraphrase Blake. The lines that follow speak of a poet's commitment to the human heart, to the different forms of desire which lend wings to our lives.

LORCA IN BARCELONA IN 1927. THE PHOTOGRAPH IS DEDICATED TO DALÍ
AND, INTERESTINGLY, IN IT LORCA DEPICTS HIMSELF AS ST. SEBASTIAN

Once again it seems that Federico is edging towards self-acceptance:

> And so, old Walt Whitman, I will not raise my voice
> Against the boy who writes
> The name of a girl on his pillow,
> Nor against the young man who dresses as a bride
> In the darkness of the closet,
> Nor against the lonely men in clubs
> Who, sick to the stomach, drink from the water of prostitution,
> Nor against men of green gaze
> Who love other men and burn their lips with silence.
> But against you, I shall cry out, city queers,
> With tumescent flesh and filthy thought,
> Mothers of mud, harpies, sleepless enemies
> Of the love that shares out garlands of pleasure.

There then follows an extraordinary piece of invective, in the form of a list of abusive terms for gays drawn from the United States, Mexico, Cuba, Portugal and a number of cities in Spain. 'Queers of the world, murderers of doves', what they all have in common is a love tainted by 'drops of foul death in bitter venom'. Gibson speculates that Lorca is railing against a great fear lodged deep within himself, namely that he too belongs to this community of the effeminate.[9] Exactly how the 'city queers' debase love, however, is not made explicit. But there may be a suggestion here that Lorca considers that they are to the ideal of love exactly what New York in the twentieth century is to Whitman's dream of community and natural order. Irrevocably defiled by materialism, these are sexual relationships that bear within themselves the stamp of their sullied world. They are part of the hostile otherness, though not for reasons of sexual orientation, but because they too conform in their own way to a uniformity of type and a shared model of behaviour. Theirs is a brashly assertive and ultimately self-regarding brand of loud and empty promiscuity which contrasts with the 'men of green gaze', an image of

Whitmanesque 'virile beauty' with which Lorca himself clearly identifies (the 'green' in this case is a common Spanish usage, denoting sexual passion). In the final analysis, the poem is a celebration of the many loves that spring from the deep well of nature and which, crucially, transcend the limitations of self and society. That homosexual love is one of these many loves should not be doubted. Lorca was so sure of it, for better or for worse, that he chose to omit the 'Ode to Walt Whitman' from the lecture which he gave once back in Spain in order to introduce *Poet in New York* to his Madrid public.

New York marked an extraordinarily prolific period for Lorca. It was an experience which not only widened his range of expression, but also gave him a hitherto unknown degree of creative freedom. Geographical distance and cultural difference, as well as the traumatic process of self-analysis upon which he was engaged, meant that he could write a poetry and theatre in New York which he knew could not be readily made public in Spain. He wrote a surrealistic film script, *Trip to the Moon,* (seen by many as a riposte to *Un chien andalou*), eventually filmed by the Catalan artist Frederic Amat in order to mark the centenary year.[10] Additionally, he worked on several plays, most notable among them the extraordinary piece known in English as *The Public* (although *The Audience* would be a more accurate translation of *El Público*). These are works which are radically experimental, kaleidoscopes of startling imagery and surrealistic detail. With them Federico achieves his desire to assert his own avante-garde credentials. The final lines of the enigmatic 'Fable and Round of the Three Friends' provide a possible allusion to this change of artistic direction (if we take his projected *Poet in New York* as his sixth major published work). Whether that is a legitimate interpretation of the lines that follow or not (and there is enough evidence to suggest that it is), it has been overtaken by their overtly prophetic nature. There are those who have argued from them that, by surrendering himself so completely to 'the chance of poetic automatism and by abandoning himself to the psychic volcanism where oracles take shape', Federico's lines provide an obscure glimpse into a dark future.[11] That is beyond any possible corroboration, but the final lines of this disturbing

poem echo a multiplicity of images of violent death that recur throughout
Lorca's work, and which are frequently associated with the poet himself:

> When the pure forms collapsed
> In the rustling of daisies,
> I understood that I had been murdered.
> They plundered cafés, graveyards and churches,
> They opened wine-casks and cupboards,
> They ravaged three skeletons to gouge the gold from their teeth.
>
> But they did not find me.
> They never found me?
> No. They did not find me.
> But still it became known that the sixth moon fled upstream
> And the sea remembered, so suddenly,
> The names of all its drowned.

Whether these lines are a statement of poetic intent, of artistic frustration, or of
a deeper sense of the self submerging under the persona of the successful writer,
it is impossible to read them without a shiver of response. To this day, officially
at least, the exact location of Lorca's final resting place remains unknown.[12]

Work to be Booed at

Lorca spent about nine months in the United States, most of it in New York,
ostensibly learning English, without any notable success. He also visited up-
state New York and parts of New England, including Vermont; an
experience recorded in about a dozen poems in the collection. In the spring
of 1930 he went to Cuba at the invitation of the Hispano-Cuban Cultural
Institute, in Havana. He was delighted to be leaving an Anglo-Saxon world
which, with the exception of the jazz-blues culture of black Harlem (a whole

section of *Poet in New York* is devoted to the blacks of Harlem), he had found simultaneously oppressive and insipid. Moreover, although he was deeply worried by the news of the Italian concordat between the Church and Mussolini (the basis for the poem 'Cry to Rome'), he was immensely cheered by the news from home that General Primo de Rivera, the so-called benign dictator, had relinquished power in order to make way for a new liberalising government. He poured all of this – joy, relief, the magnetic attraction of Cuba, his lifelong love of Cuban music – into the poem with which *Poet in New York* is brought to a close, 'Music and Sound: the Negroes of Cuba'. It is a poem which captures perfectly the rhythms and sounds of the *son*, the traditional Afro-Cuban musical form, and as such it provides not a colophon to *Poet in New York*, but its joyous antidote. Federico was back on Hispanic soil, in a culture he could recognize as being similar to his own.

New York represented a double catalyst for Lorca, bringing two ongoing but as yet unresolved crises to a head. Firstly, instead of the lonely sublimation of his own sexuality into his writing, he now begins to investigate and probe it through his work, and in doing so begins to develop the notion of a real and undefeated (rather than lost and defeated) community: the blacks of Harlem, the 'comrades' of Whitman. A Freudian introspection begins to give way to a Kleinian search for community. Secondly, no doubt in some way as a result of his experience in the fragmenting world of a capitalism that was wholly alien to his spirit, he also began to interpret and express the contemporary urban (rather than timeless rural) world in and through the disturbed and disturbing imagery of his own inner turmoil. It is a form of writing which shares much of the surface characteristics of surrealism, but although much of the imagery remains puzzling, there is an emotional coherence in the poems, an intelligibility of personal reference, which prevents this writing from sliding into free-form association. It was perhaps therefore inevitable that around the same time his thoughts should have turned to a new type of theatre: radical in its conception, fragmented and jarring in characterization and development, and dealing openly with homosexual themes, virtually for the first time in Spanish theatre. Ground-breaking then in every sense. Small wonder that Lorca should have referred to *The Public* as a play 'to be booed at', predicting, correctly, that it would never be performed in his lifetime. Both the theatre and public attitudes towards homosexual love have had to grow considerably to accommodate the vision of this innovative and demanding play.

It's quite possible that Lorca began to think about *The Public* when he was still in New York – although the evidence suggests that most of what actually exists of the play was written in Cuba. Originally described as a play in 'twenty scenes and a murder', only six (not necessarily chronological) scenes have appeared to survive. However, given the play's rejection of anything remotely like a storyline, it is impossible to speculate with any degree of certainty as to how Lorca intended to finish the piece (if indeed he himself knew). In many ways, this is a play about the nature of theatre itself. At the centre of *The Public* is the tension between the 'theatre of the open air' and the 'theatre beneath the sand', that is, between the commercially centred aesthetic of the Director with his safe and traditionalist representations of life, and the design of a convulsive, shocking theatre which probes below the surface of conformism and fear (Lorca had already established the link between pervasive fear and sand in 'Ballad of the Spanish Civil Guard'). The theatre beneath the sand, the play of deep-seated emotions and desires that fracture conventional attitudes and expression alike, announces its intention to turn the stomach of a bourgeois audience hidebound by certainty and narrowly defined tastes. Theatre's responsibility to its audience is to shatter conventional morality, to advance sensibilities and knowledge, even if that advancement marauds into the realms of the scabrous, the scatological and, of course, the sexual:

> DIRECTOR: *What moral is there to all of this? And what about the spectators' stomachs?*
> MAN 1: *There are people who vomit when an octopus is turned inside out and*

there are others who go pale when they hear the word 'cancer' spoken in a certain way [...] But what you're doing is to deceive us. To deceive us so that nothing changes and so that we can do nothing for the dead.

The theatre beneath the sand will explode the layers of restraint and codified thinking, which in *The Public* are represented by the psychosocial motif of the mask. The Director defends theatre's masking of the terrible truths, its clothing of the unpalatable in 'the silks of the poet's bedroom':

In the middle of the street, the mask buttons us up and avoids the unwise flush which sometimes rushes to our cheeks. In the bedroom, when we stick our fingers in our noses or delicately run them over our arses, the plaster mask squeezes our flesh so tightly that we can hardly lie down on the bed.

The mask helps us to avoid the occasion of sin, defined for us not as a spiritual imperative but through the squeamish morality of the status quo. A status quo whose own model of love is exemplified by the conventionally romantic staging of *Romeo and Juliet* (a story whose deep and hidden passions fascinated Lorca and which, barely a couple of years later, he was to retell in *Blood Wedding*). Juliet is one of the kaleidoscope of lurid and poetically conceived characters who appear in *The Public*. But she too is the victim of conventional views of love:

WHITE HORSE 1: Juliet, the night is not a moment, but a moment can last all night.
JULIET: That's enough. I'm not going to listen to you. Why is it me you want to take? It's all lies, the word of love, the broken mirror, the footstep in water. Afterwards, you'd put me back in my grave again, like everyone else who tries to convince anyone who'll listen that real love is an impossibility. I'm tired of this and I've risen up to ask for help in expelling from my grave all those who theorise about my heart and all those who prise open my mouth with little marble tweezers.

Later she will confess her love for the horses, for these 'real horses who [...] have shattered the stable windows'.

I'm not frightened of you. You all want to go to bed with me, don't you? But now it's me who wants to go to bed with you, but it's me who says so, me who directs, me who rides you, me who cuts yours manes with my scissors.

The castration image may well reflect Lorca's personal unease as to dominant female sexuality. But the quotation also captures one of the central intentions of the play as a whole. The force and shape of desire is a uniquely individual expression, and when it is brought into the open air it shatters the conventional constructs of gender. *The Public* proudly announces the 'very last truly feminine Juliet that the theatre will see'.

A School for Desire

Like the 'Ode to Walt Whitman', *The Public* gives voice to human desire in all its forms. A desire that inevitably leads to perversion, understood not as a moral judgment, but as the breaking away from the established codes and conventional manifestations of sexuality and gender. It is a perversion which leads us straight into the heart of the struggle, the confrontation between the socialized and the instinctual, which had preoccupied Lorca throughout his artistic life. The politics of desire were to exercise Lorca's creative imagination for the rest of his life. This is not to say that upon his return from New York he was to throw himself wholeheartedly into the creation of a body of work whose primary line of engagement was social or political. But the poet clearly saw in drama the opportunity to speak to an audience, to create the community from which, throughout so much of his life, he had been excluded. The emotive charge of theatre, and of tragedy in particular, could serve to create a pre-political consciousness in the spectator. In particular, at a time when women were given the vote for the first time, he

was acutely aware of the political need for them to see as clearly as possible the stranglehold which male self-interest had placed round their lives.[13] In the theatre he created after his return from New York, family life, marriage and property are condemned as pillars of a repressive ideology. Lorca's analysis leads him to a clear awareness that the double-standards implicit in gender relationships are the function of economics. Along a very different route, he has arrived at a position which parallels that of Engels and Marx. Four of Lorca's best-known plays, *Blood Wedding, Yerma, Doña Rosita the Spinster* and *The House of Bernarda Alba*, written in the four years between 1932 and 1936, all depict the tragedy of the conservative woman. He is imparting the bitter lessons he has learnt since adolescence, hoping to create the same pre-political consciousness in women that his repressed sexuality had driven home in him.

It is as if, having emerged from the artistic cauldron of New York, Federico has mustered the emotional strength to begin to diagnose his own illness, to interrogate the otherness which has both confronted him externally as a system of hostile social codes but which has become part of him, the result, above all perhaps, of parental attitudes. And to recognize that this illness, this otherness, has a public dimension; Lorca's dedication to the mainstream theatre in the last four years of his life is rooted in his realization that what he is telling is not solely a private issue (although this is the level at which it is inevitably experienced with greatest pain), nor simply a metaphor for cultural marginalization, but that it is an historical trauma whose roots and whose potential development are all wholly identifiable both within a Spain asserting its future in the face of entrenched traditionalism, and a Europe sliding through growing authoritarianism towards conflict.

In early 1935 a special performance of Lorca's new play *Yerma* was arranged in Madrid's Teatro Español for an audience of actors and directors. He addressed them with a manifesto which gives eloquent testimony to his awareness of the social responsibilities of the theatre:

The theatre is a school for laughter and tears, an open forum where we can put ʊ or misguided moralities to the test and embody in living examples the eternal tru of the human heart.[14]

There are three related issues here: the idea that theatre can and should reorientate the spectator towards what Lorca considered to be the most precious fulfilment of one's being: the emotions; that theatre had a role in the debate between modernization and traditionalism raging at that time in Spain; and that performance is the key to an impact which derives from emotional response but whose goal is fundamentally an advancement of knowledge.

Lorca's description of the theatre as a school reflects the general cultural project of Republican Spain. The more utilitarian aspect of this is seen in Lorca's acceptance of the commission to direct La Barraca, a student group whose remit was to bring the classics of Spain's Golden Age to the towns and villages of the country. As a talented director and lucid dramaturg, Lorca clearly identified the central issue of Golden Age theatre as the clash between desire and the law, dramatized as a primary issue of public concern, and this further sharpened his sense of theatre as a place where the explicit politics and moralities of the law should be put to trial and the invisible politics and moralities of private desire given a public airing and explored in terms of both social control and intimate crisis.[15]

As a result of the advancement of diagnosis and the strengthening of resolve which was New York, Lorca's rural trilogy establishes his hitherto loosely defined sense of hostile otherness in terms of recognizable sociopolitical patterns of traditional Spain and of the authoritarian consciousness. For example, it is clearly important to *Blood Wedding's* status as ritualistic drama that the inevitable failure of the young lovers who attempt to break free from their rigidly coercive society is seen as not solely the result of star-crossed destinies, but that it has also been brought about in some way by the archetypal father and mother figures (who together represent the powerful

DRESSED IN THE TRADITIONAL BLUE BOILERSUIT OF LA BARRACA,
LORCA ADDRESSES AN AUDIENCE BEFORE A PERFORMANCE

working of tradition). But the mother and father are also identifiable in terms specific to their time and place, the father as a caricature of greed for land, the *pacto de la sangre con la tierra*, the blood-bond with the land which has been a major item of faith in Spanish traditionalism, and the mother as the chilling voice of a society without peace, without reconciliation. It is the father's lust for land which occasions the break-up of Leonardo's relationship with the Bride before the action proper of the play even begins, and it is precisely the Mother's obsession with the knife which leads her to virtually placing it into her son's hand as she drives him out from the Wedding in pursuit of the wayward lovers. The *navaja* ('knife') is a recurring sign in Lorca's poetry, plays and drawings, taken, as are so many of his motifs and icons, from the immediate physical world. If one were translating the force of the word into an Irish situation, then its direct equivalent would be 'the gun', and it was precisely this sense of a real place inhabited by real violence which the Irish poet Brendan Kennelly develops in the last few lines which he appends to his version of *Blood Wedding*.[16] Both knife and gun are readily intelligible correlatives for a certain type of social and historical violence, both potent agents and harbingers of a destruction whose causes are known to all. In other words, the first mention of the *navaja*, highlighted as it is at the beginning of the play, creates a shiver of expectation as the audience confronts the tragedy of a relentless chain of cause and effect which it recognizes as being its own trauma.

Lorca's determination to probe a heart of darkness which is simultaneously specific to his culture and universally human leads him inevitably to unmask the nothingness, the absence of value, which lies at the heart of the authoritarian consciousness, dramatized with remarkable force in *The House of Bernarda Alba*. Absence and negation are powerful elements in Lorca's dramatic universe. Where they are most powerfully evoked is through his poetry, that living poetry which is of the stage, when characters speak from the very heart of their being. Which means that Lorca's plays are no less difficult for Spanish audiences than they are for an English-speaking one. The poetry of his original Spanish texts has, in performance, something of the effect of an estrangement – specifically, perhaps, in the way in which Brecht described his *Verfremsdungeffekt* as 'the things of everyday life lifted out of the realm of the self-evident'.

It seems curious to mention Lorca and Brecht in the same breath, but Lorca's experience of New York had led him to a deep conviction that what makes life most precious is also most absent from the codes of our living. Unlike Brecht, however, Lorca does not superimpose an estrangement effect on his theatre in order to prompt the spectator towards a rigidly rational analysis. Rather he is concerned to speak directly to his spectator's emotions so as to subvert the spurious stranglehold of reason, to strengthen the private self in its battle with the imperatives and dictates of the public. Paul Valéry, a poet admired by Lorca, insists that poetic language is essentially concerned to negate our most ingrained values and codes of behaviour, speaking only 'of absent things'. This is exactly the achievement of the richly imagistic drama which was being written by Lorca in the 1930s. It is a theatre which disrupts established patterns of conformist behaviour with forceful expressions of the intimate self, of the right to be, beyond all morality and all theology. Lorca's characters, in the deepest expression of their intimate being, inhabit an amoral and godless universe.

Lorca would have had no difficulty in seeing as a statement of politics his own expressed view that the goal of life is happiness. To give voice to the silenced self, the yearning for an absent happiness, is to challenge the established order of things, to imply a different way of being. It was Gabriel Marcel who noted that 'through the emotions I discover that this concerns me after all', and through the *duende* of performance the spectator is ineluctably drawn into a shared community of emotion. The real artistic achievement of the rural tragedies is the creation of what Marcuse thirty years later was to call a 'non-reified language', that is, a form of expression which not only restores the individual's right to subjectivity, but which through that challenges a world whose guiding norm is the spirit of negation.[17]

Speaking the Silence

The defining element of this theatre is the confrontation it provokes with the absences and negations operating within the intimate life of each spectator. There can be no doubt that Lorca's rise to prominence in Britain in the 1980s is in great part due to the response at that time to this dramatic project, the redefining of community via the formal equivalent of an audience united through the democracy of the emotions rather than the elitism of intellect.[18]

As a Thatcherite society increasingly defined the individual in terms of the freedom to acquire, many turned to Lorca's vision of the individual defined in terms of the dissident extension of selfhood. The playwright's experience of naked materialism in New York, the pursuit of money at the expense of life (the image of a stockbroker hurling himself from an office window haunted Lorca), and the heaving crowds in which individuals seemed willingly to sink their identity ('Poem of the Vomiting Multitudes' and 'Poem of the Urinating Multitudes') were, in their way, a prefigurement of radical monetarism. The lesson was not to be lost.

Lorca's later theatre is, in every sense, primarily about making what is invisible or repressed in society visible on stage. The boldness of much of Lorca's theatre, particularly after New York, is that it imagines woman with pleasure as her object, and that that object is sexual. Why Lorca should be concerned with the sexual as a site for oppression is obvious. And as what is being made visible on stage is desire, felt and expressed as an imperative of nature, then that desire transforms itself into a force wholly intelligible within the particular codes and repressions of the individual spectator. In other words, Lorca's plays speak simultaneously of hetrosexual male, female *and* gay sexuality, because they are above all else a vehicle which gives voice to the force of desire. Pleasure and desire move from the realm of abstraction into the domain of passion; they are not simply named but re-created through the force of poetry, and that is how they are experienced by the audience. What was unspeakable before has now been given voice.

At the heart of this theatre is the radical exposition of difference, of deviance from the law. Lorca is more concerned to deconstruct the essentials of this culture than he is to celebrate them, dramatizing its social and political pillars and moral imperatives as a single force of hugely hostile otherness – from the institution of marriage, the absorbent sense of community, the relentless capitalist ethic of work and acquisition, to the driving aspiration to reputation (the honour code). Lorca never seeks to minimize the cohesive strength of these forces − dramatized linguistically through inanimate strands of imagery, such as glass or stone, scenically as walls that divide and exclude, and cosmically, most forcefully perhaps in *Blood Wedding, through the* conspiracy of the Beggar Woman and the Moon. He has been all too aware, from the first burgeoning of his sexuality, that society has a relentless capacity to manipulate and control the subversive world of the instincts. His stay in New York, his confrontation with urban modernity, also taught him that society can find ways of sublimating this world through alternative schemes of production and acquisition. And as it does so, it atrophies the individual's capacity to grasp the alternatives. This is the real lesson that Leonardo wants to teach the Bride in the forest scene of *Blood Wedding*. His simple disavowal of the community imperative − 'if I thought as others do' − unmasks the assumption that it is society which is the real, the rational. This is the rebirth of the individual consciousness outside the productive apparatus, outside the social codes, outside tribal memory, outside language as the agent of a universal moral thought to which personal feelings and capacity for independent action must be surrendered. In the anonymity of New York, Lorca has seen how easily consciousness is obliterated by reification, by the inherited consensus of the general necessity of things. Of course, the Bride eventually returns to the community, but the ultimate meaning of *Blood Wedding*, like all of Lorca's plays, is located not in its narrative line, but in the form of its telling, in its poetry.

In terms of the relationship between theatre and the individual consciousness, Lorca's work prefigures some of the central developments in radical cultural theory that were to take place after his death. His is a coherent interrogation and cogent deconstruction of authoritarianism and of the reified consciousness that political analysts and social philosophers like Wright Mills, Marcuse or Read decades later were to identify as lying at the heart of contemporary disaffection. Through the poetry of his plays, however, he also permitted his audience to feel and to grasp alternatives. This is what makes Lorca's later theatre genuinely subversive: its emotional charge is the foreshadowing of a different way of being.[19] To grasp the alternatives is, of course, both to understand the contradictions and lament the apparent impossibilities. This is what theatre has been doing since Aeschylus, and Lorca was always fully aware of the great truths of the tradition of tragedy from which he saw himself as deriving and to which he sought to contribute.[20] But after New York, his tragic sense was a distinctly modern one. Moreover, as his fame grew throughout the 1930s, most notably with hugely successful productions of *Blood Wedding* throughout Spain and in Latin America, he began to make a number of public statements which revealed his sympathy for the forces of change and modernization. His famous remark, for example, that he had more in common with a 'good Chinaman than a bad Spaniard' was a conscious sideswipe at right-wing nationalism. He was rapidly establishing a reputation as a radical whose sympathies lay with the left, a tag which seemed justified by the fact that there is a perceptible sharpening of the political overtones of the themes and basic situations of both *Yerma* and *The House of Bernarda Alba*. In the final analysis, however, Federico was never really a political thinker, let alone an activist. But at the time, as the two Spains began to square up to each other with the silent connivance of a Europe preparing for its own conflict, perception was everything. Lorca was an intellectual, sexually subversive – the rumour was spreading in some circles that he was an 'invert' – and the author of apparently overtly political pieces like 'Ballad of the Spanish Civil Guard'. To be truthful, he did allow himself to mimic the polarized mood of the times in some of his declarations to the press:

> For as long as there is economic injustice in the world, the world will be unable to think with any clarity [...] The day hunger is wiped out, there will be the greatest spiritual explosion of all time. We'll never be able to imagine the joy there will be come the Great Revolution. I sound like a real socialist, don't I?

There is undoubtedly some explicitly political posturing here. But his most deeply felt commitment was to what Sean O'Casey, just a few years earlier, had called the 'divine mission of discontent'. By making his audience complicitous with the struggle for love and freedom of a whole series of female protagonists – the Bride, in *Blood Wedding*, Yerma, Adela, in *The House of Bernarda Alba* and Doña Rosita, destined to die a virgin having been abandoned a lifetime before by her fiancé – the dramatist is not only providing a version of his own struggle, but is also demanding a critical analysis of a culture in which such things are possible. But Lorca rarely gives any idea of where specifically he would like that analysis to lead. It was not his job to do so. Moreover, he had not resolved the crises in his own life, despite his by now massive literary reputation. One of the last plays he was working on in 1936, now known as *Play Without a Title*, is set in a theatre at a time of civil disturbance. It certainly indicates that he was becoming increasingly preoccupied with the relationship between theatre and politics, but the play seems to suggest that politics belongs to what was called in *The Public* 'the theatre of open air'; it is a distraction from the real business of life – and death.[21]

The Author in *Play Without a Title*, unlike his counterpart, the Director, in *The Public*, is very much an artist. In Lluís Pasqual's world premiere of this hitherto unknown piece, in Madrid in 1988, the action was fleshed out by scenes from *A Midsummer Night's Dream*, which the Author is endeavouring to stage for his public. In common with all tragedians, Lorca was fascinated by the ever-present possibility of the unforeseen that, in an instant, can cut away the solid ground from under our feet. *Poet in New York* and *The Public* are both full of images of abrupt and arbitrary transformation; *A Midsummer Night's Dream* similarly provided a startling image of the capacity of love to turn even the strongest will to jelly (a theme that also lies at the centre of *Blood Wedding*). Federico had had every reason to feel himself at times no more than the puppet of his passions. The warning sounded by the Author in *Play Without a Title* is that theatre must address the truths that are locked away, otherwise our lives will become written wholly in superficial fictions. In one of the greatest moments of *duende* in the whole of Lorca's theatre, he reminds his protesting audience that instead of the politics of the open air, they should

be preparing to face the truths beneath the sand:
Even the youngest of you in this room should know that the wood from which your coffin will be made has been cut and already lies drying.

Once again, life is put into the perspective of death; the only perspective which truly sharpens the appetite for living.

It is quite possible that the unruly audience in *Play Without a Title* (the piece ends with the actual storming of the theatre) was based on Lorca's experience during the premiere of *Yerma*, in 1935. As usual the first performance of any piece by the man who by that stage was considered the country's foremost dramatist aroused a great deal of public and critical interest. Some of that interest was predictably hostile, especially so when the author was seen moving in circles close to the Republican left (most specifically Manuel Azaña, just released from prison for political activities and soon to become the last socialist Spanish Premier before the Civil War). Snippets of information about the subject matter of the play which leaked into the press also served to whip up feelings. In the event, the opening performance, attended by the whole of Spain's cultural establishment (including Luis Buñuel who later declared himself 'unimpressed'), did not attract an uprising on an Abbey-like scale. But there were loud protests from the traditional right, and the word 'pansy' was hurled at Lorca from the auditorium. What was more worrying was the hysterical reaction in the right-wing press which viewed the play as a blatant attack on Spanishness itself. To some extent, of course, they were right, but the venom of the reviews, with hindsight, can be seen as a clear indication of a country that was growing increasingly divided against itself. However, the production was counted a huge success by virtually everyone, that is, except for the Catholic right and the surreal-blinkered Buñuel.[22] But if anyone in Spain had been in doubt as to Lorca's apparent political affiliations, then these doubts seemed to have been dispelled once and for all. It is worth stressing again that when a society becomes divided against itself, perceptions are the only reality that count.

None of this prevented Lorca from talking with his characteristically engaging blend of enthusiasm and fantasy about future projects, of new works to be staged and new works to be written. Foremost among these were his desire to see *Doña Rosita the Spinster* staged in Madrid after its hugely successful run in Barcelona, and to dust off a play written in 1931, the diamantine, but still unstaged, *When Five Years Pass*.[23] This latter piece, subtitled with characteristic Lorquian care as a 'Legend of Time in Three Acts and Five Scenes', is recognized by many as among his most innovative and effective pieces of writing for the stage. More coherent than *The Public*, but also more strikingly expressionistic than any of the rural tragedies or *Doña Rosita*, the play distinguishes in a characteristically Lorquian way between our deep needs (in this case, once again, love) and the false consciousness that conventional views place upon us. The fact that all of this is set in the framework of the rapid flow of time gives the work an additional poignancy. A Young Man postpones for five years the consummation of his great love for his fifteen-year-old fiancée. In the final analysis it is, of course, never consummated, and the young man meets his death in an absurd and meaningless way. He is accompanied throughout by the Old Man, who is a constant reminder that there is but the thinnest of spans between youth and old age, and that we must with some urgency make and take our memories rather than postpone them. It is a lesson which also underpins *Doña Rosita*, and it is interesting to speculate on Federico's questioning through these two plays of his ingrained fear that inaction might be preferable to discovery.

Nothing is Heard but the Weeping

There is another reading which one can take from *When Five Years Pass*, one which deepens the personal dimensions of a work about which Lorca was unusually silent. The Young Man's postponement of marriage is not just an idealistic rejection of the sensuous Friend who tells him 'I prefer to eat her green or, even better, to cut her flower and wear it in my lapel'. For this Fiancée is no simple flower waiting to be plucked, but a complicated woman of equally strong appetites who 'waited naked, like a serpent of wind' for her lover to return. There are some suggestions in the play that it is precisely this aspect of his fiancée's sexuality which terrifies the Young Man; that what he is in fact postponing is not the moment of consummation, which could only occur when his bride to be had achieved her majority, but rather the act of consummation itself.[24] This supplementary reading is further enforced by the hallucinogenic scene near the beginning of the play in which a Cat appears with a Dead Child, an externalization of the future sterility which faces the Young Man. In this way, a commonly held view of the play is that Lorca is still working through the implications of his separation from the world of heterosexual love.[25] But *When Five Years Pass* is a hybrid work. On one hand, the influence of and competition with Dalí and Buñuel is clear in the play's rupturing of the forms and planes of reality. On the other, however, unlike *The Public,* its exploration of the hostility of time to love is wrapped not in Lorca's most direct experience, but in a more publically acceptable (if somewhat thin) heterosexuality.

His unprecedented success in the theatre in the last five years of his life did not mean that he abandoned poetry. Indeed, during that time he wrote some of his finest and most mature poems. One of these is the powerful elegy, 'Lament for Ignacio Sánchez Mejías'. Sánchez Mejías was an extraordinary figure by any standards, a bullfighter who was also a novelist, playwright and flamenco devotee, with a deep interest in the new psychoanalysis.[26] Federico was fascinated by him both because he shattered the normal expectations held of that typical icon of Spanishness, the bullfighter, and because his bisexuality challenged the traditional schism between male and female forms of sexuality. In 1934, however, against every scrap of good advice that came flooding his way, Sánchez Mejías was tempted back into the ring for one final fight after several periods of retirement. The ring was Manzanares, and this *corrida* was indeed to be his last. When he heard of his friend's death, Federico apparently told a friend that 'Ignacio's death is like mine, the trial-run for mine'.[27] He immediately set about writing an elegy whose emotional key is never strained, but captures beautifully the anger, pity and fear, as well as the moved recollections, that come in the train of bereavement. Written in four sections – 'The Tossing and the Death', 'The Spilt Blood', 'The Body Present' and 'The Soul Absent' – the poem demonstrates Lorca's ability to construct a classical elegy (this poem contains virtually all of its conventional elements - initial disbelief, abiding horror, eulogy etc.) while at the same time communicating his own very individual sense of tragedy and its consolation. Although he could not bear to see the body of his lifeless friend, the poem itself is pitiless in its confrontation with the finality of death. But there is a final consolation, as there must always be. It is the consolation both of art and memory through their lyrical re-creation of what has gone. It is a lesson which those who sometimes dismiss Lorca's theatre as negative and depressing would do well to remember. These are the final lines of the poem:

> Then autumn will come like a spiralling shell
> With misted grapes and clustered hills,
> But no one will want to look into your eyes
> Because you have died for ever.

> Because you have died for ever
> Like all the dead of the earth,
> Like all the dead who are forgotten
> On a forgotten heap of rotting dogs.

> No one knows you. no. but i sing of you.
> I sing of your profile and your grace.
> The maturity of your thought.
> Your appetite for death and the taste of its mouth.
> The sadness that lies beneath your valour's smile.

Much time will pass before such an andalusian is born again,
If ever is born one so noble.
I sing of his elegance with words that moan
And I remember a sad breeze among the olive trees.

The poem was published the following year. The other major books of
poetry which Lorca was working on during this period were not to see the
light of day so quickly.

Since his return from New York, Federico had been working on a collection
which, in the first instance he apparently intended to call *Poems for the Dead*,
but which, when it was given its first public reading in 1935, was entitled *The
Divan of El Tamarit* – *divan* meaning a collection in Arabic, and El Tamarit
being the name of his uncle's estate just outside Granada. The collection is
composed of two Arabic forms, the *caside* and the *gacela*, both of them
traditionally used for erotic poetry. Lorca, however, puts them to a wider use.
These are some of the most powerful of Lorca's poems, in the sense that their
linguistic simplicity and directness of image allows the reader a penetrating
insight into the dark complexities of his emotional world. Underlying many
of these poems is the brooding threat of violence and morbid fascination with
death. Death as an end of everything, except perhaps the mysterious world of
dream, of memory and of art. From the 'Gacela of Dark Death':

I want to sleep the dream of apples,
To leave far behind the tumult of cemeteries.
I want to sleep the dream of that child
Who wanted to cut his heart on the high seas.

I don't want them to tell me again and again
That the dead do not lose their blood,
That their rotting mouths still ask for water.

I don't want to know of the ordeal by grass
Nor of the moon with her serpent's mouth
Who works in the silence just before dawn.
I want to sleep a while,
A while, a minute, a century;
But let everyone know that i have not died,
That there is a stable of gold on my lips;
That I am the little friend of the west wind;
That I am the immense shadow of my tears.

From the perspective of New York, Lorca had grown sharply aware of the dangers confronting Europe. He had witnessed the rise of fascism, his Civil Guards moving relentlessly from the realm of myth to that of history. And he must have at the very least intuited the violence to come in his own Spain. The 'Casida of the Weeping' is not the battle cry of the political poet; it is the lament of the poet who cannot escape from his commitment to suffering humanity:

I have shut my balcony
Because I do not want to hear the weeping,
But behind the grey walls
The only thing that can be heard is the weeping.

There are very few angels who sing,
Very few dogs that bark,
A thousand violins fit in the palm of my hand.

But the weeping is an immense dog,
The weeping is an immense angel,
The weeping is an immense violin,
The tears bind the wind
And the only thing that can be heard is the weeping.

Finally, the *Sonnets of Dark Love*. This suite of 11 tightly written poems is much more than an exercise in form, as the poet's brother was to claim (in the absence of the evidence of the manuscript itself).[28] They are the record of another love affair and, specifically, of a journey to Valencia and Cuenca undertaken in 1935. These poems speak of the explosion of love in the poet's body and emotions. Their tone is quite different from the *Divan* poems, as once again he takes refuge in intricate codes and hermetic seals in order to protect his vulnerability. But there is no doubt that the 'loved one' in these poems is male; the unavoidable grammatical necessity in Spanish of making adjectives agree with nouns makes that quite clear. The 11 poems explore and celebrate the daily miracle of the lover's presence, the joy and anguish of letters and telephone calls, the sharing of a bed, love-making in the dawn etc. The sonnet form and the echoing of the language of Spain's greatest love poets of the Golden Age – Garcilaso, Quevedo and Góngora – do not conceal, however, the fact that the rich conceits of these secretive poems unravel into the awareness that when love is a madness, then this is the most bitter of all madnesses. 'Wounds of Love' characterizes his passion variously as 'this weight of the sea pounding me' and 'this scorpion dwelling within my breast'; it is not a passion to be embraced with simple willingness. It is a passion he could not avoid. The Bride's long speech of justification in the final scene of *Blood Wedding* springs immediately to mind. Here is the final tercet of the poem:

> And though I seek the height of prudence,
> Your heart offers me a valley stretching
> With hemlock and bitter knowledge.

Excessive orthodoxy creates dissidence in its wake. Federico was not the willing embodiment of a searing passion. Like so many of his characters, he simply couldn't get out of its way.

Part of it was, of course, the age-old problem of reputation. In the play that he was writing at about that same time, Bernarda Alba's house is a fortress of oppressive codes surrounded, in her imagination at least, by a forest of wagging tongues. This is the play in which the *el que dirán*, the 'what the neighbours might say', is at its most destructively pervasive. Although Lorca vehemently detested with equal force the voice of social censure and the caving in to it, he was himself by no means wholly immune to its pressures. Otherwise, he could not have invested *The House of Bernarda Alba* with the force of truth that gives the play such powerful balance. 'The Beloved Sleeps on the Poet's Breast' is clearly based on an unpleasant incident, presumably in a hotel, when the lovers are spied on or baited by others. Pursued by 'a voice of penetrating steel', the poet can only urge his lover to sleep, as downstairs polite society dances the night away:

> But sleep on, my love, sleep on.
> Listen to my blood break against the violins,
> And watch how they lie in wait for us still.

Perhaps the poem which best encapsulates the dilemma between the joy of physical love and the accompanying sense of personal destruction is the, initially at least, disjointed 'Oh Secret Voice of Dark Love'. The poet is torn between the voice of secret desire and the fear of the loss of reputation and literary name ('the hard marble of my head') that an openly homosexual relationship would undoubtedly occasion:

> Oh secret voice of dark love!
> Oh bleating without wool! oh wound!
> Oh bitter needle, sunken camelia!
> Oh current without sea, city without walls!

> Oh immense night, secure of shape,
> Celestial mountain high with anguish!
> Oh voice pursued, a dog in the heart!

Silence without end, mature lily.
Let me be, hot voice of ice,
And do not ask me to lose myself in the dark undergrowth
Where flesh and heaven moan without fruit.

Leave the hard marble of my head,
Take pity on me and break this grief!
For I am love, I am nature!

Images of confusion, of love constrained, of nature denied and the resultant emotional turmoil, precisely and passionately recorded. Above all else, what animates this poem is his anger that he should be torn between the imperatives of his nature – indeed, his natural rights – and the desire to escape from all it, to return to uncomplicated living.

In the event, however, Federico did find an all-consuming love in the final couple of years of his life, with Rafael Rodríguez Rapún, the man who was in all likelihood both object and recipient of the beautiful *Sonnets of Dark Love*. Rapún had previously been secretary to the student theatre group, La Barraca, which Lorca directed upon his return from New York. Shortly afterwards, he became Lorca's own personal secretary. There is very little more to tell. Both covered their tracks with remarkable care. No documentary evidence of a relationship survives, although Rapún was probably the beloved of the *Sonnets of Dark Love*. History records that exactly a year to the day after Federico was murdered in Granada, Rodríguez Rapún was killed in battle in Santander, in the north of Spain.[29]

TAKEN IN THE HUERTA DE SAN VICENTE, GRANADA, IN THE LAST
YEAR OF LORCA'S LIFE

Death in Granada

The Dark Root of the Scream

The causes of the Spanish Civil War are too intricate and numerous to enumerate here.[1] What was clear was that throughout the first six months of 1936 Spain was growing increasingly polarized, and that events within Europe were steadily piling more fuel onto the process of embitterment and division. The tension reached breaking point in the early summer of that year, in the wake of a number of political assassinations carefully calculated so as to destabilize an already volatile situation. Lorca read the writing on the wall with frightening clarity. '[...] these fields are going to be strewn with corpses! My mind is made up. I'm going to Granada, come what may', he told Rafael Martínez Nadal.[2] And against the advice of his friends, he travelled back to his home city on 14 July 1936, to be with his family for the celebration of the saint's day that he shared with his father.[3]

Barely four days after Federico's arrival at the Huerta de San Vicente, however, General Franco and a number of other right-wing generals brought their conspiracy to its bloody conclusion. The Civil War began in earnest. It wasn't long before the whole of Andalusia was in nationalist hands, unleashing a wave of political reprisals and sheer fascist terror. Lorca could not have felt himself immune from the dark terror of officially sanctioned repression that was taking place around him. Moreover, although he had endeavoured to be discreet, his presence in Granada had clearly been noted. By the end of the first week in August, it seemed only a matter of time before he too would be taken by the terror gangs operating officially and unofficially in and around Granada.[4] He apparently discussed the possibility of trying to pass over into the Republican zone, but finally opted to go and stay in the house of a friend and fellow poet, Luis Rosales. He was confident he would be safe there, for they were a well-known nationalist family. Indeed, Rosales and his brothers were members of the extreme-right Falange Party. But it was all to no avail. For whatever the reasons – anti-intellectualism, envy, hatred for his homosexuality, resentment, the willingness to believe that his writings were a political campaign against Spain rather than a moral one against ingrained inhumanity – he was taken from his refuge on 16 August, rapidly processed through a kangaroo court and, in the early hours of the 18 August, he was shot by military firing squad on the road between Viznar and Alfacar. His body was tossed into an unmarked pit, alongside the three other men – a republican school-teacher and two anarchist bullfighters – who had been executed with him. A few bucketfuls of lime were scattered on top as though to conceal the crime from history.[5]

As news of his death spread, a number of friends blamed themselves for not having insisted on Federico leaving the country with them – to Mexico, Italy, France, among other destinations. Quite clearly, returning home to Granada proved to be a literally fatal miscalculation. It is idle to speculate on the deeply rooted reasons which took Lorca back to his family at that very dangerous time. But deep-rooted reasons there must have been, for he had dramatized the homing instinct in a number of plays, most notably in *Blood Wedding*. Here the Bride, having just witnessed her lover and jilted bridegroom stab each other to death, thinks only of returning to the house of her Mother-in-Law in the village. Of course, her situation is quite different. In such a society, there are few public spaces open to the wayward woman, unless it is the brothel. But, at least from her perspective, she goes back from a position of strength. This is one of the most remarkable things about an extraordinary play. She goes back to where she belongs. Her attempt to build a new life based on love, rather than on the empty contract of marriage, has failed; she returns to her blood community. In a similar way, perhaps, Federico never achieved that alternative community, his version of Whitman's almost mystical camaraderie, which he needed in order to construct his own spiritual home. Throughout his writings, a number of his characters welcome a moment of stasis when the violence of life is raging all around. He too returned to the stasis of home, to his own, at a time of crisis. But his own were surrounded by those who had been, and who remained, hostile to his very presence. Stasis was gone for good.

As he waited in the Huerta de San Vicente in those final days, it is quite likely that he would have put some finishing touches to his most recent play, *The House of Bernarda Alba*. It is easy to see the final word of that play, the cry of 'Silence!' uttered by a Bernarda Alba who is refusing to acknowledge the pain of her daughter's suicide, as darkly prophetic. For a sort of silence did indeed gather round Lorca's work in Spain until many years after his death. And of course his murder was the infliction of the ultimate silence. But Lorca was primarily identifying a broad-based reality, a society's refusal to confront its deepest truths. The tension between silence and the scream is one of the defining elements of his work. At the end of *Blood Wedding*, Bride and Mother speak the following words:

> Neighbours, it was with a knife,
> Just a little knife,
> That on the appointed day between two and three,
> Two men in love killed each other.
> With a knife,
> Just a little knife,
> That fits snug in the hand
> And slices so quickly through the startled flesh
> To stop at the point
> Where, trembling enmeshed,
> Lies the dark root of the scream.

The scream is the only possible response to a silence which has rendered ordinary speech useless. It is a reaction beyond words to a suffering beyond bounds. In some ways, Lorca's most deeply personal works, *Poet in New York* and *The Public*, both raise screams which seek to convulse existing forms and shatter the deafening silences. But all of his work is about the telling of truths that have been locked away. In the words of Yerma:

> *There are so many things locked away behind these walls that if they were suddenly to go out into the air and scream, then the whole wide world would fill with their shrieks.*

Perhaps this is what we finally take away from the work of Lorca: the sense of its commitment to speaking the unspoken, to giving voice to what lurks only half-recognized or repressed under the surface of our socialized selves. It is a body of work which is constantly challenging boundaries; the boundaries of our emotional experience, of sexuality, even of gender itself. Above all perhaps it challenges the boundary between thought and imagination, creating as it does so often the powerful and unique poetry which comes when people speak from the very centre of their being: the 'stable of gold' on the poet's lips.

Notes

Preface

1.   See, for example, *The Unknown Federico García Lorca*, edited and translated by John London (Atlas Press. London, 1996). Contains dialogues, dramatic projects, unfinished plays and the filmscript of *Trip [Voyage] to the Moon*. *Play Without a Title* is also included here as *The Dream of Life*. It is translated by Carlos Bauer as *Play Without a Title* in Federico García Lorca, *Two Posthumous Plays* (New Directions, New York, 1983). The other play in this book is *The Public*.
2.   Literally, 'what a terrible shame!'.

Introduction

1.   This forms the Prologue to Lorca's *Obras Completas [Complete Works]*, Vol.2, (Aguilar, Madrid, 1980). The first edition, with a number of very serious lacunae, was published in 1954.
2.   See, for example, Paul Julian Smith, *The Theatre of García Lorca: Text, Performance, Psycholanalysis* (Cambridge University Press, Cambridge, 1998).
3.   Ian Gibson's contribution to Lorquian studies has been immeasurable. See especially his *The Death of Lorca* (Paladin, St. Albans, 1974) and *Federico García Lorca. A Life* (Faber, London, 1989). The former was reissued as *The Assassination of Federico García Lorca* (Harmondsworth, Penguin, 1983). The latter book is an excellent and detailed biography, itself a translation and condensation of the two-volume biography published by Grijalbo (Madrid, 1985 and 1987).
4.   Nicholas Round, Introduction, Federico García Lorca, Four Major Plays, translated by John Edmunds (Oxford World Classics, Oxford, 1997). The four plays are *Blood Wedding*, *Yerma*, *The House of Bernarda Alba* and *Doña Rosita the Spinster*.
5.   See Marcelle Auclair, *Enfances et mort de García Lorca* (Seuil, Paris, 1968), 417.
6.   Andrés Sorel, *Yo, García Lorca* (Zero, Bilbao, 1977), 203. Written in the wake of Gibson's pioneering *The Death of Lorca* (which by that time had caused a stir in Spain), this book sets about re-evaluating Lorca's life and work in the context of the transition from Francoism

to democracy.

7.   Gibson, *The Death of Lorca*, 136.

8.   Fernando Vázquez Ocaña, *García Lorca. Vida, cántico y muerte* (Grijalbo, Mexico, 1962), 349. He clearly believes that he is defending his dead friend from defamation of character.

9.   Eulalia-Dolores Higueras Rojas, *Mujeres en la vida de García Lorca* (Nacional, Granada, 1980), 52. The title of the book [*Women in the Life of García Lorca*] is decidedly ambiguous, as Angel Sahuquillo suggests in his *Federico García Lorca y la Cultura de la homosexualidad masculina* (Ensayo e Investigación, Alicante, 1991). In this context, Sahuquillo quotes from the New York poem 'Infancy and Death': 'Here all I see is that they've closed the door on me/ they've closed the door on me'. Sahuquillo's book, while curiously bitty in its structure, is the most complete analysis to date of Lorca's work from the perspective of his homosexuality. As far as I am aware, it has not been translated into English.

10.   Rafael Martínez Nadal, *Lorca's The Public. A Study of His Unfinished Play and of Love and Death in the Work of Federico García Lorca* (Calder & Boyars, London, 1974). See also Preface, Note 1.

11.   Daniel Eisenberg, 'Reaction to the Publication of the *Sonetos del amor oscuro*', *Bulletin of Hispanic Studies*, 65 (1988), 261-271.

12.   *Federico García Lorca (1898-1936)* (Lorca Centenary Commission, Madrid, 1998). In all other respects, a remarkably complete and well-documented catalogue.

13.   See also Paul Julian Smith, 'A long way from Andalusia', *TLS* (August 7, 1998), in which he compares the Granada commemoration with the fiesta-conference held at Newcastle Playhouse in May–June 1998.

The Fall from Grace

1.   For a readable introduction to the work of the Generation of '98, see Donald Shaw, *The Generation of 1898 in Spain* (Benn, London, 1975).

2.   See Introduction, Federico García Lorca, *Yerma and The Love of Don Perlimplín for Belisa in he Garden,* translated and introduced by David Johnston (Hodder & Stoughton, London, 1990).

3.   Gibson, *Lorca*, 15.

4.   Gibson, *Lorca*, 15.

5.   Gibson, *Lorca*, 15.

6.   Gibson, *Lorca*, 15.

7.   See, for example, Federico García Lorca, *Selected Letters*, translated and edited by David Gershator (Marion Boyars, London, 1984).

8.   Taken from 'La vida de García Lorca, poeta' an interview which took place in 1934, and published in Vol. 2 of the *Obras Completas*.

9.   See Note 8.

10. See *Federico García Lorca, Blood Wedding*, translated and introduced by David Johnston (Hodder & Stoughton, London, 1989).

11. Reproduced in Vol. 1 of the Obras Completas. See also Introduction, Johnston, *Blood Wedding*.

12. See Paul Binding, *Lorca. The Gay Imagination* (GMP, London, 1985), esp.31–32. A ground-breaking book in English.

13. Hamish Henderson, 'Lorca and *cante jondo*', Cencrastus (Summer 1987), 6–10. This piece is particularly interesting in its attempt to find some sort of cultural and linguistic equivalent for the idea of *duende*.

14. See Introduction, Johnston, *Blood Wedding*. Binding tends to impose a rather Anglo-centric viewpoint on this aspect of Lorca's work (Gay Imagination, 164).

15. Gibson, *Lorca*, 39–40. It seems likely that his subsequent determination never to appear effeminate has its roots in the pain occasioned by such taunts.

16. See, for example, Ramón Sainero Sánchez, *Lorca y Synge, ¿un mundo maldito?* (Universidad Complutense, Madrid, 1983).

17. There is an English-language translation of *Impressions and Landscapes* in existence, although even in Spain it is rare to come across the work outside the pages of the Obras Completas. See *Impressions and Landscapes*, translated and edited by Lawrence Klibbe (UPA, Lanham, 1987).

18. There are clear parallels here with the early work of D H Lawrence. See, for example, Anthony Burgess's *Flame into Being. The Life and Work of D H Lawrence* (Heinemann, London, 1985).

19. There are several anthologies of Lorca's poetry available in English. The earliest and least successful is *Selected Poems*, introduced and edited by J L Gili (Penguin, Harmondsworth, 1960). Some of the most readable translations are to be found in one of the most recent: *Federico García Lorca, Selected Poems*, a bilingual edition translated by Merryn Williams (Newcastle, Bloodaxe, 1992).

20. See Binding, *Gay Imagination*, esp. 51.

21. See Sahuquillo, *Cultura de la homosexualidad*, 20–22.

22. Music was of crucial importance to Lorca. A number of different recordings of his songs, as well as of his poems set to music, are readily available. Interestingly, the *Sonnets of Dark Love* first came to popular attention in Spain through the musical arrangements of the well-known Leonese singer/composer Amancio Prada.

23. See *Deep Song and Other Prose*, translated and edited by Christopher Maurer (Marion Boyars, London ,1980).

24. The lecture is reproduced in its entirety in Williams, *Selected Poems*.

25. The whole issue of the performability of Lorca in translation is debated in *Donaire* (Winter, 1998), a journal published by the Consejería de Educación (the Education Office of the Spanish Embassy), 20 Peel

Street, London.

26.   See Introduction, Johnston, *Blood Wedding*.
27.   See Introduction, Johnston, *Blood Wedding*.
28.   Binding, *Gay Imagination*, 173.
29.   Sahuquillo, *Cultura de la homosexualidad*, 20–22.
30.   Lorca took his drawing very seriously, and showed his work, for example, in Barcelona. For an insight into this dimension of his multi-faceted talents, see Helen Oppenheimer, *Lorca. The Drawings* (The Herbert Press, London, 1986). In this context, see especially the section entitled 'Drawings concerned with personal identity'.
31.   For a full treatment of the causes of Lorca's crisis at this time, see Gibson, *Lorca*, 205–241.
32.   Federico García Lorca, *Poet in New York*, translated by Greg Simon and Steven F White, edited by Christopher Maurer (Harmondsworth, Penguin, 1990). See Introduction, xxvi.
33.   See, for example, Binding, *Gay Imagination*, 19–20.

The Realm of Law

1.   It is only in recent years that the Islamic contribution to Spanish history has been evaluated positively. Traditionalist readings have tended to attribute the anachronistic aura that all too often surrounded Spain to its prolonged contamination by 'Africanism'.
2.   See Agustín Sánchez Vidal's *Buñuel, Lorca, Dalí: El enigma sin fin* (Planeta, Barcelona, 1988), esp.35–46. This is a well-researched and engaging book. Unfortunately, it has not been translated into English.
3.   Luis Buñuel, *Obra literaria* (Heraldo de Aragón, Zaragoza, 1982), 241.
4.   Quoted by Sánchez Vidal (*Enigma*, 24) from Robert Descharnes, *The World of Salvador Dalí* (Macmillan, London, 1962). The retranslation is mine.
5.   In an interview with Lluís Permanyer, in the Spanish edition of *Playboy* (January 1979). Also quoted by Sánchez Vidal (*Enigma*, 25–26).
6.   Dalí and Lorca in fact planned a book entitled the *Book of Putrescent Philistines* (see Gibson, *Lorca*, 141 and 162). In their second cinematic collaboration, *L'age d'or*, Buñuel and Dalí announced their intention as being that of attacking 'a society in a state of putrefaction', a phrase drawn in turn from the Surrealist Manifesto. It is likely that the widespread use of the term in the Residencia de Estudiantes has its origins in the Manifesto.
7.   Luis Buñuel, *Mi último suspiro* (Plaza y Janés, Barcelona, 1982), 64. Translated into English as *My Last Breath*.
8.   Buñuel, *Suspiro*, 144.
9.   Buñuel, *Suspiro*, 64–65. See also Sánchez Vidal, *Enigma,* 47–49.

10. Sánchez Vidal, *Engima*, 49.
11. Lorca was introduced to puppetry while still a youngster. Some of his early experimental pieces for the stage are written for puppets, while the figure of the puppet itself clearly provided a good metaphor for his view of people who are the puppets of their passions or of the forces of social control. For one of Lorca's best puppet plays, see *The Puppet Play of Don Cristóbal*, included in *Lorca. Plays: Two*, translated and introduced by Gwynne Edwards (Methuen, London, 1990).
12. Sánchez Vidal, *Engima*, 158.
13. Sahuquillo, *Cultura de la homosexualidad*, 18-19.
14. Sahuquillo, *Cultura de la homosexualidad*, 19.
15. Sahuquillo, *Cultura de la homosexualidad*, 19.
16. Sánchez Vidal, *Engima*, 265.
17. Alain Bosquet, *Entretiens avec Dalí* (Belfont, Paris, 1966), 54. A series of fascinating interviews. Much of the information and opinion is repeated in autobiographical works like *The Great Masturbator*.
18. Gibson, *Lorca*, 161.
19. Sánchez Vidal, *Engima*, 125.
20. It is quite likely that Lorca enjoyed a brief love affair with Luis Cernuda in the late 1920s. Cernuda, a brilliant if very different poet, went into exile at the time of the Civil War.
21. The moon is one of Lorca's most potent images, frequently representing death (as its appearance in the final act of *Blood Wedding*, one of the most potent scenes in the whole of Spanish theatre). But the moon is also presented in terms of sexual ambiguity (in the same scene in *Blood Wedding*, for example, the Moon is played by a pale, young woodcutter). Once again, the link between death and sexual ambiguity.
22. For many of the reasons outlined here, I included this poem as a song in my version of *Yerma* (see Johnston, *Yerma*).
23. A version of *The Basil-Watering Girl and the Prying Prince* is included in London, *Unknown Lorca*.
24. Translated into English by Robert Havard, and published by Aris & Phillips.
25. For an English-language translation of *The Butterfly's Evil Spell*, see Edwards, *Lorca. Plays: Two*.
26. For an English-language version of *Don Perlimplín*, see Johnston, *Yerma*. The version   published here has been adapted as the libretto of Simon Holt's opera *The Nightingale's to Blame* (premiered in 1998).
27. See also Paul Julian Smith, 'A long way from Andalusia', *TLS* (August 7, 1998).
28. The *Romancero gitano* has been translated into English by Robert Havard as *Gypsy Ballads*, and published by Aris & Phillips.

29. This is a line aluded to by Arturo Barea, one of the pillars of the old
     Spanish left, in his now widely criticized (but still readable and, in
     places, perceptive) early study of Lorca: *Lorca: The Poet and His People*
     (Faber, London, 1944).

Desire and Perversion

1.   In a note to his friend, Carlos Morla Lynch. See Gibson, *Lorca*, 245.
2.   Juan Larrea, 'Asesinado por el cielo', *España peregrina* (Mexico, 1940),
     251.
3.   Introduction, Federico García Lorca. *Poet in New York*, translated by
     Ben Belitt and introduced by Angel del Río (Grove Press, New York,
     1955), xiii–xiv.
4.   There are now several different translations of these plays available. In
     addition to the ones noted above, see also Gwynne Edwards' *Lorca:
     Plays One* (Methuen).
5.   The text of this lecture is reproduced in English in Maurer, *Poet in
     New York*, as is a selection of some of Lorca's letters to his family
     written from the New World.
6.   There are further parallels with D H Lawrence here. Like Lorca, the
     English novelist knew all about sexual frustration, like Lorca he too
     dramatizes/novelizes escape from these frustrations through suicide,
     and like Lorca he too frequently takes solace in the construction of a
     panerotic principle intimately connected with the earth.
7.   Sahuquillo, *Cultura de la homosexualidad*, 109–111.
8.   The section on this poem is one of the highlights of *Lorca. The Gay
     Imagination* (see especially, 131–142).
9.   Gibson, *Lorca*, 297–298.
10. The filmscript is composed of 73 images, tending to the surreal. Image
     5 is interesting: 'Letters spelling the words "Help, Help, Help", rising
     and falling as they are superimposed over a woman's sexual organs'
     (My translation). For the complete script, see London, *Unknown Lorca*.
11. Del Río, *Poet in New York*, xxix.
12. From Del Río, *Poet in New York*, x: '[Conrad Aitken] saw a warning in
     "the recurring preoccupations of this book – pain, pain and suffering,
     fear of death and injury, the agony of the conscious mind in the
     presence of universal pain... There has been no more terribly acute
     critic of America than this steel-conscious and death-conscious
     Spaniard, with his curious passion for the modernities of nickel and
     tinfoil and nitre, and for the eternities of the desert and the moon. He
     hated us, and rightly, for the right reasons"'.
13. See Patricia McDermott, 'Yerma: Extra Naturam Nulla Salus', *A Face
     Not Turned to the Wall* University of Leeds, Leeds, 1987). McDermott
     notes that the 'title-name Yerma [...] firmly establishes the protagonist

as the feminine *tierra española*, scenario for the spiritual civil war
between nature and culture, Love and Law, freedom and repression' (237).

14. See Introduction, Johnston, *Yerma*.

15. Lorca's versions of some Golden Age plays were also performed with
notable success in theatres in Madrid, Barcelona and even Latin
America. A notable example is Lope de Vega's comedy *La dama boba*.

16. Kennelly's version was performed at the Newcastle Playhouse, and
published in Bloodaxe (1997). He clearly had the Northern Irish peace
process in mind in the final lines he appends to the play.

17. There are many parallels to be drawn between Lorca's sexually
subversive writings and the revolutionary thought of Herbert Marcuse.
See, especially, Marcuse's *One Dimensional Man*.

18. Arnold Wesker has suggested that the sustained popularity of Lorca in
Britain derives from the fact that the definition and acceptance of
certain areas of the social role of women remains problematic even
today. This echoes the reason behind the initial popularity of Lorca's
theatre in Spain after the death of Franco. See Arnold Wesker, 'Nuria
Espert abre las puertas de Londres a Lorca' in *Insula*, 3 (Madrid,
October 1985).

19. The emotional truth of performance is a version of the truth of the
alternative ways of being and of seeing the world which the work
seeks to impart. See also Marcuse, *The Aesthetic Dimension*.

20. 'Lorca's concept of tragedy has its origins in his sexuality, which must
have led him not only to question the way things are but to believe
that he was somehow fated'. Commentary, Federico García Lorca,
Blood Wedding, translated with Commentary and notes by Gwynne
Edwards (Methuen Student Edition, London, 1997), xxxv.

21. The central idea of the inauthenticity of the political in contrast to the
philosophical issues surrounding the fabric of life and death is implicit
in the play's alternative title, 'The Dream of Life'. See London, *The
Unknown Lorca*.

22. See Gibson, *Lorca*, 396–399 ('Yerma scandalizes the Right').

23. Translated as *When Five Years Pass*, in Edwards, *Lorca: Plays Two*.

24. See, for example, Gibson, *Lorca*, 314–317.

25. 'In the void that is at the center of his swirling images, in the eye of
the storm, in the resonant hollow of the well, is an absent child'.
Maurer is referring to *Poet in New York*, but this remains one of the
great lacks in Lorca's life. See Maurer, *Poet in New York*, xxiii–xxvii.

26. The 'Lament' is translated in Williams, *Selected Poems*.

27. See Binding, *Gay Imagination*, 179.

28. Federico's brother, Francisco, wrote a biography under the title
Federico y su mundo, translated into English by Christopher Maurer as
In the Green Morning: Memories of Federico (Peter Owen, London,
1989). Francisco's introduction to his brother's theatre was also

included *per force* in the official translations published by Penguin, until the moment of deregulation in 1986.

29. Gibson comments on Rapún's death: '[...] a sudden air attack caught them unprepared. Unlike the other men Rapún did not throw himself to the ground but remained sitting on a parapet. A bomb exploded nearby and he was mortally wounded' (471–472). The implication is that Rapún was so distraught on the anniversary of his lover's death that he had no wish to survive. Surely, in this context, Gibson's remark that 'Lorca – and it seems impossible that Rapún could have been aware of this – had been assassinated a year earlier to the day' is a misprint.

Death in Granada

1. For one of the most readable accounts of the causes of the Spanish Civil War, see Gerald Brenan, *The Spanish Labyrinth* (Cambridge University Press, Cambridge, 1960).
2. Gibson, *Lorca*, 443.
3. The saint's day (after whom one takes one's name) is celebrated with as much joy as one's brithday. When father and elder son shared the same name, as in this case, the celebration would normally have been momentous.
4. For full details of the repression in Granada, see Gibson, *The Death* and *The Assassination*.
5. Luis Rosales has always insisted that he went to the military headquarters to try and secure his friend's release. For many years, however, there were those who whispered that Rosales had been somehow involved in Lorca's arrest. Letters came to light not long after Rosales's death, however, which proved his absolute innocence.